PRAISE FOR

PRAISE FOR
BUILT THROUGH COURAGE

"Dave Hollis shares life-changing guidance to help you get through seemingly insurmountable challenges and come out the other side a better, stronger you."

—MARIE FORLEO,
#1 *New York Times* bestselling author
of *Everything is Figureoutable*

"*Built Through Courage* will see you through the storms of life and help you harness the full unleashing of your greatness. It's a must for anyone looking to connect to their true purpose."

—TRENT SHELTON,
author, motivational speaker,
and founder of Rehab Time

"A TrimTab is a small rudder that moves the large rudder that moves the ship. This book can be a TrimTab for you if you let it: reading this can change the direction and trajectory of your life."

—GREG MCKEOWN,
host of the *What's Essential* podcast
and two-time *New York Times* bestselling
author of *Effortless* and *Essentialism*

"You know that you are meant for more, but you can only discover what 'more' is if you are following your own life map. Dave Hollis knows this better than most, and he has put together the incredible lessons he has learned the hard way, so you don't have to. Get ready to get clear on what's next in your journey!"

—NATALIE and DANIELLE CANTY,
founders of Bossbabe

"Dave Hollis gives us unfiltered access to the ups and downs he has faced over the last couple of years. His is the voice you need to hear when you're low, encouraging you to chart your own course and build a life for yourself, rather than for someone else."

—LEWIS HOWES,
New York Times bestselling author
and host of *The School of Greatness*

"If you've ever felt lost, untethered, or afraid to move forward because of your past, this book is for you. Recounting the breakdowns that led to the breakthroughs, Dave Hollis guides you on a journey, weaving story and tangible takeaways in a way that allows you to take inventory on where you are and to ensure that where you're going is a far more compelling place. This book is filled with hope, renewal, and an honest look at how you can build your own life brick by brick through courage."

—JENNA KUTCHER,
host of *Goal Digger Podcast*

"Dave Hollis approaches *Built Through Courage* with great honesty and introspection. He shares his years of experience and unique perspective to explore what it truly takes to create a fulfilling life." —MIKE BAYER, two-time *New York Times* bestselling author and CEO of CAST Centers

"Dave Hollis has a grip on navigating life not because he is perfect at it, but because he is purposeful at it. Through this book, I've found that in order to rescue my life from mediocrity, I must risk having a life of bravery. Risk in order to rescue. Dave shows us the way." —CARLOS WHITTAKER, author, speaker, and hope dealer

"I've known Dave Hollis for years now. I've seen him navigate a thunderous rollercoaster of extraordinary highs and difficult lows, but through it all he has dazzled me with his humility, poise, and courage. Every now and then you meet someone who swears they're just stumbling through life, learning as they go. But as you watch them, you realize that their stumbling looks better than most people's dancing. Dave is that guy, and I'm proud to call him a friend." —TOM BILYEU, CEO of Impact Theory

"When you read this book, it's easy to imagine Dave Hollis out at sea on a sailboat. There's a storm on the horizon, but he's just unfurled the one thing that will add peace and promise to the entire journey: a map. 'Here's where we are. Here's where we're going. Here's how we'll get there!' he shouts over the waves, with a vulnerability and sense of hope that's contagious. If you find yourself stuck on the shore and you know it's time to leave the harbor for deeper waters, start with *Built Through Courage*." —JON ACUFF, *New York Times* bestselling author of *Soundtracks*

"Dave Hollis is the epitome of courage. The courage this man has to always show up as his true self is not an indication that it's easy—we all know it's not!—but an example that when it's tough—in fact, especially when it's tough—we *can* do it. We just have to be willing to leave the safe harbor. And if you decide you are ready, then this book is your adventure guide and Dave is the captain. All aboard!" —LISA BILYEU, cofounder of Impact Theory

"If you're looking to find your path and your place in the world, along with the courage to follow it, Dave Hollis's lessons and vulnerability to dig deep and share his own journey will inspire your own!" —JAMIE KERN LIMA, *New York Times* bestselling author of *Believe IT* and founder of IT Cosmetics

BUILT THROUGH COURAGE

FACE YOUR FEARS TO LIVE THE
LIFE YOU WERE MEANT FOR

DAVE HOLLIS

HarperCollins
Leadership

AN IMPRINT OF HarperCollins

Published by HarperCollins Leadership, an imprint of HarperCollins Focus LLC.

Any internet addresses, phone numbers, or company or product information printed in this book are offered as a resource and are not intended in any way to be or to imply an endorsement by HarperCollins Leadership, nor does HarperCollins Leadership vouch for the existence, content, or services of these sites, phone numbers, companies, or products beyond the life of this book.

Book design by Aubrey Khan, Neuwirth & Associates.

ISBN 978-1-4002-3066-2 (eBook)
ISBN 978-1-4002-3066-2 (HC)

Library of Congress Control Number: 2021944000

Printed in the United States of America
21 22 23 24 25 LSC 10 9 8 7 6 5 4 3 2 1

CONTENTS

SECTION 1
WHERE YOU ARE

SECTION 2
WHERE YOU ARE GOING

FOR JACKSON, SAWYER, FORD, AND NOAH

may you always have the courage to step
fully into who you were meant to be

DEAR READER

FEAR HAS BEEN the strongest and most consistent emotion of my entire life. I grew up the most afraid kid in school, where worry was my love language. I'm willing to admit that, long after school ended, fear was still there, running the show. I say this to acknowledge that the decision to write a book about cultivating courage is something that makes me a little self-conscious when I think about the contrast of who I've been. The way I've given power to fear throughout my life.

I've been a mix of good and bad, strong and weak, disciplined and inconsistent. I've had seasons of life where I was extraordinarily proud of the way I showed up, and plenty of times in the past five years where the challenges of stepping into who I was meant to be brought out things that weren't my best. My mistakes were often fueled by fear. Usually in desperate need of courage to course correct.

There is only one way that I can help you understand how to create the courage you'll need for the life you deserve: by talking honestly about the times when being courageous produced good outcomes as well as when a lack of courage kept me in my own way. We're all on a journey of becoming better versions of ourselves, and the way learning from my mistakes has helped me become a better, stronger version of me is a thread throughout the pages ahead.

This book is about having the courage to face the fears of leaving your safe harbor for a purpose-filled life. The idea that pushing away from comfort and cultivating the courage to do something that scares you in the attempt to honor the intention of your creator isn't so much an option, but a requirement for anyone interested in a life of growth, fulfillment, and impact.

As I write this book, I am the absolute best version of myself. That's vain and true. I am sitting on the other side of three significant voyages from my version of a safe harbor into the chaotic and choppy seas where growth would forge this best version of me. A harrowing journey into foster care and adoption, the decision to leave the entertainment business and my seventeen-year career at The Walt Disney Company, and the transition from being married to divorced.

In each case, the discomfort of leaving behind what I knew well was an invitation to become something greater. To move away from suffering I'd clung to because of its familiarity. To break down muscle so that it might be built back up stronger. By holding tightly to the correlation between leaning into the choppiness of new waters for the benefits that would come in my evolution, it's afforded me a confidence to be even more courageous in pushing beyond the boundaries of my comfort zone any time something new begins to feel like something normal.

That said, stepping into my calling still leaves me with doubts. I'm human after all. In fact, I had a conversation with my therapist about my ambition to create resources and tools in books and coaching, but that I worried my not-all-together self might not be totally equipped for this work. He turned the conversation on its head.

"Is there a chance that because of the work-in-progress that you are that you're perfectly qualified to talk to people about taking steps to get whole?" he asked. "Could your journey of discovery, even as it's messy, be something that permits someone else to take a step forward in their messiness?"

Yes sir. I believe these words to be true, and even as I'm myself still on this journey that you're on, we'll do this imperfect, messy work together. It feels important to set the record straight up front—that's what you're getting here. Someone who knows what it is to face the prospect of swimming into choppy waters. Someone who is nowhere near all together, believing in the mandate to heed the call, choosing to be brave even though it's scary and exhilarating and daunting. Because it's where true fulfillment lies.

So climb aboard. This voyage is a mix of storytelling and frameworks. It's passive reading and active learning prompts. It's the things that worked for me in the hope that you can discover what will work for you. As much as I'll share aspects of my wiring, my faith, my perspective, and my experiences, even as you think, believe, or act in ways that are different from me, my hope is that this work serves as a catalyst to help you find the best ways to cultivate courage in your life. The courage you'll need to become who you were created to be.

Let's go.

Dave

INTRODUCTION

UNMOORED

*A ship in harbor is safe,
but that's not what ships are built for.*
—JOHN A. SHEDD

I HAVE THIS quote tattooed on my right forearm. It is my mantra, a constant reminder that the life I want exists outside of my comfort zone. The only way I can evolve into the person I want to be for myself and for my family, someone who is proud of himself when alone in his thoughts, is by pushing beyond what is easy and familiar. It requires challenging myself, every day, to journey into unknown waters, even when I am afraid. It demands that I decide to do it scared and am willing to learn from the mistakes that will inevitably come with new experiences.

I'm not good on boats. I've never loved the open water and I tend to get seasick. It may seem funny that someone who dislikes boats would have a quote about ships tattooed on their arm or would choose to write a book with a nautical theme. And yet I've done this in the name of challenging my comfort zone. By nature I tend to feel most comfortable anchored and close to shore. I prefer the safety of the harbor to the chaos of waves and weather. I know what it is to be *stuck*, to rationalize being just okay, because it feels safer than putting myself out there and challenging the status quo.

We're all victims of a harbor in which we find ourselves anchored. The stories we've been told, the societal constructs in which we live, the fear that governs our willingness to cling to the suffering that we know—it all exists as a framework that constrains how we *become*. This book in part is an attempt to confront the allure of the dock. The appeal of the anchor. I argue that although we're designed as a ship built for the high seas, we often trade off the benefits that come from the choppy waves for the safety of calm waters. Yet the waves lead to growth that sits as the foundation for our fulfillment.

Many of us struggle with pushing beyond our comfort zones, but we must rise to the challenge of embracing the uncomfortable, of doing what scares us. This is a lesson that I want to teach my four kids. In fact, this is why I got my tattoo: as a constant, indelible reminder of what I want to impart to them. I want them to know that in order to unlock their true gifts, they must own who they are, and they must bravely sail out of the harbor to explore the places that challenge them and create growth. We can convince ourselves a thousand times over to settle for good, but we deserve great. On days when we doubt ourselves and our ability to navigate rough waters, we must return to this truth: We were made for this. Like boats built to weather the storm, we already have everything we need inside of us to handle the discomfort that comes from living into our calling.

•   •   •

This past year has been the hardest of my life. This past year has been the best of my life.

It is strange to think that those two things can coexist, but I am here to tell you that it's possible. In fact, the growth that feels the hardest and is the most painful is often the most important.

At the end of 2019, I declared that 2020 was going to be my best year ever. At our company holiday party, just ahead of my forty-fifth birthday, I made this proclamation from the DJ booth we'd rented in a small event space outside of Austin while acknowledging where I was starting from: a feeling of being a bit unsteady as a first-time author, first-time coach, first-time podcast host. First-time everything. But I knew where I wanted to go. I had a plan for the year. I would become the *captain* of my ship as I steered toward the waves. This is how my year would unfold:

I'd kick things off by running a marathon.

Then I'd launch my book with a thirty-city tour.

Then I'd continue building a company with my wife and partner, with whom I'd host a morning show and a successful podcast, as we balanced it all with four kids and a house in the country.

One of those things went the way I'd thought it would. I ran the marathon.

As it turned out, 2020 had other plans for everyone, but for me, this is what it looked like: My book tour was canceled. I transitioned away from the company I'd built with my wife, where I'd imagined working for the rest of my career. And I watched my sixteen-year marriage, which I had never once considered ending, unexpectedly dissolve. All of this was compounded by a global pandemic, followed by a long overdue racial reckoning, a tumultuous presidential election, and everything else the year brought us collectively.

It was the hardest year of my life, wildly outpacing any previous hard year. One filled with grief and sadness, identity crisis and a broad sense of loss. But it also turned out to be my best, as you will come to see.

* * *

At that holiday party, where I'd boldly declared that I was on the brink of my best year, we'd invited an on-site poet, Liz Garton Scanlon, to take a word that each of us was sitting with and turn it into a keepsake. My word was "unmoored." I knew that I was preparing to untie from the dock and hit the high seas, and I was feeling the discomfort of my decision. The same uneasiness I felt embarking on an adoption journey into the unknown four years earlier. Similar to the disorienting feeling I experienced leaving my role as president of sales at Disney two years earlier. The same discomfort I'd come to feel in my marriage ending just months after she wrote these words.

Liz wrote this poem for me:

Unmoored

for Dave

Ropes are not as perfect as they seem to be when you first spy a solid square knot.

Rope burns are not uncommon, in fact.

So you untie, throw caution to the wind (and boy, howdy, is there wind)

And also tides

And storms

And serpents

But when you tip over the edge of the world,

hiking halfway up the hull and the gulls scream with glee

and the sun comes up again and again and again?

You do not miss the rope at all.

I had made a declaration that I was about to embark on my best year ever, but I wouldn't get to dictate the sea conditions. It turned out that getting to my best would require weathering the worst climate of my life, one that began as a tropical storm then quickly became a hurricane followed by another hurricane, and another after that. The entire time I was navigating those impossible seas, I remained stable by reminding myself that becoming the true captain of my ship wasn't something that calm water could produce.

As Franklin Roosevelt said, "A smooth sea never made a skilled sailor."

• • •

So why are you here?

Why did you pick up this book, of all the books on the shelf, and all the authors you could choose to spend your time with? Perhaps it was because you have been through a difficult period yourself, and you are looking for a way forward. Perhaps you are looking for a friend, and some guidance, as you try to get yourself unstuck. My hope is that in spite of the challenges you are facing, you feel that same tug inside that I do. That little voice nudging you to keep asking questions about how you can live a fuller, richer life. My hope is that this book will help you to determine what a fuller, richer life means for you, so that you can develop the courage to sail through the rough waters ahead and chase that life you want. And I hope that you will come to understand that you are worthy of and ready for this kind of life. I hope that, through this journey we're on together, you will develop a deeper understanding of where you are now, where you want to be, and what it's going to take.

As much as I want this book to be a resource for your personal development, there's something about many of the books on the personal development shelf that rub me the wrong way. Often, I will be reading or listening to something that feels like a prescription: just do these things and you will be happy and whole. That's a hard pill to swallow. I just don't think it works that way. I don't buy into a one-size-fits-all solution, because I believe that each of us must follow a path that is specific to who we are, where we want to be, and who we hope to become. And I hope that through our work together, you will find your own unique way of navigating these waters.

This will require, up front, that you believe you are built for these seas. It will require you to understand that taking a step into the unknown will come at the expense of your comfort, but that your willingness to invite discomfort will be precisely why you'll grow through it and become the person you are meant to be.

A ship in harbor is safe, but that's not what ships are built for.

You were built for this.

It's time to leave the harbor.

A POWER GREATER THAN YOURSELF

There is something bigger than us in every storm we face. You may call it God or Buddha or Allah, or you may chalk it up to intuition, the universe, or some sort of Jedi magic. It's that profound feeling in your gut that's trying to get your attention, that seemingly already knows something you need, the direction you should take, even as it might not yet be completely clear to you. It's that tug on your heart, a longing in the recesses of your soul that, no matter how hard you fight to quiet it, it just won't go away. When you connect to it, listen to it, make a relationship with it, you appreciate that the outcome ahead is not exclusively in your hands. The question is: Can you open yourself up to willingly consider that the whisper you hear repeated in the depths of your being already knows how you'll make it through? It's there, pleading, in the hopes you'll finally believe it enough to listen.

An important piece of this journey is trusting in a power greater than yourself to be your guiding force. Letting go of the need for a tidy explanation for everything that happens to you and around you. You wouldn't be reading this book if there wasn't some part of you that was curious about how your version of bigger, better, and more fulfilled might come to be. The courage required to free your rope from the dock is cultivated in the one-two punch of belief in yourself and connection to something far greater than you.

As a parent to four kids and a four-time foster parent, there have been countless times when I believed in their ability to do something before they fully believed it themselves. If you're a parent, I know the same is true for you too. Consider a toddler's first-step moments when the curiosity born out of watching their model has them teetering upright, hand on that coffee table, ready to make a first step. As you start shouting, "You can do it! Come on! Walk to me! Take that step!" you're affording that toddler *borrowed belief*.

It starts with you as an external force giving that baby some confidence, but you don't need to understand the biology of childhood development to appreciate that something greater than their skills or your influence is also responsible for the child's ability to walk. Your wisdom and experience as a walker lights a fuse that fosters their exploding into something they were intentionally designed for. It's that combination of faith and design that allows them to take that first step. And then another.

It reminds me of a story in the Bible when Peter sees Jesus walking on water and says, "If it is you, command me to come on the water." With the simple command of, "Come," Peter does something he didn't think he was capable of, pushing aside doubt and conventional thinking as he borrows the courage of his faith. Courage from the command.

He gives his limiting beliefs, his anxieties, and his insecurities over to a higher power. He believes he's that ship built for the choppy waters, and in that belief leaves his own harbor. The implication of the command: he was prequalified for the task. He does something he previously would never have thought possible for himself.

He walks on water.

But then, the wind picks up. The voices in Peter's head express doubt and drown out the promise of his caller. Peter sinks. Underwater. Gone.

Like all of us, Peter was human.

It is as true today as any time it's been declared in the centuries since: God doesn't call the qualified. He qualifies the called.

None of us have it all together, yet all of us have been called to "come" at some point in our lives. Be it from the parent who saw in you an ability to walk, an employer who has high expectations of you, a significant other who partners with you to build a life together, even a close friend or family member who knows you can accomplish your dreams. You have been called to come into spaces that are beyond your comfort zone, where you can evolve into who you were created to be. To come away from your long familiar suffering. To come toward growth. Yes, there are creatures and swells and unknown dangers that live in that water beyond the harbor, but it's in those waters where you'll find the things you've been looking for.

As we begin this journey, taking that first step may make just about as much sense to you as it did to that baby teetering on newly found legs. In other words, it might not make any sense at all. But when we have faith in ourselves, faith in a power greater than our own, faith in the possibilities that exist beyond our comfort zone, all that is required is that we muster the courage to take that first step. And then another.

When we commit to taking those initial steps, we set ourselves on a path toward something greater. We begin the journey toward who we have the potential to become. But it's not for the faint of heart. Peter walked on that water until the winds blew. In the work that lies ahead, there's plenty of wind.

THE PERSPECTIVE OF EXPERIENCE

One of my hopes in this book is that you will see yourself in some of my stories. That sharing my experiences, feelings, and thoughts may give you something of an empathy bridge that normalizes your struggle, honors your evolution, and encourages you to keep going. Especially when we're early on in our journey or find ourselves stuck, there's something powerful about being able to see the way that someone else with experience is afforded the benefit of perspective, and how that perspective can offer us belief and hope in ourselves. A wink and a nod to keep us going, like the experienced walker shouting encouragement to the beginner on wobbly new legs.

One of the coolest parts of my job at Disney was the opportunity to attend screenings, along with other Disney execs, and provide feedback on unfinished, unreleased films to the filmmakers. As much as I consider myself to be a creative human, in my role at Disney, I leaned more on an analytics team than on my imagination to help me make decisions and strike deals. The idea of me providing storytelling insight to the creative talent at Disney is almost laughable. And yet . . .

In my first year as sales head, when I was naïve enough not to fully understand how these feedback sessions worked, Disney had a distribution agreement with DreamWorks Pictures, the live-action film studio helmed by arguably the greatest filmmaker of all time, Steven Spielberg. Yes, this is going to go as badly as you're imagining.

In 2011, Mr. Spielberg made *War Horse*, a World War I epic that was ultimately nominated for six Academy Awards. The film is a beautiful, emotional, harrowing depiction of the ravages of war. I was excited by the opportunity to see the film and absolutely loved it. When I returned to my office, I got a call from my boss.

"Don't forget. You need to call Steven and let him know what you thought."

Totally normal. Not freaking out. "Will do."

When we got on the phone, I told him how much I enjoyed the film, the score, the cinematography. I gushed over the emotion, the amazing performances. All good. And then I offered an unsolicited filmmaking recommendation to the three-time Academy Award winner that *Time* magazine has called one of the one hundred most influential people of the century.

"You know, there's that sequence where the shot is beautifully capturing the deserters fleeing through a sweeping windmill before you hear the gunshots and they fall dead? I just wonder if that being in the film doesn't make it harder for us to sell this to families at Christmas when the picture comes out?"

Without missing a beat, he said, "You know, Dave, when I made *E.T.*, I was on the talk show circuit promoting the opening and I was asked by an interviewer why in the world I had Elliott say the words 'penis breath' in the dinner sequence. Why would I do that to a family movie? And the answer was simple. I left it in because that's what happens at family dinner tables. And while I appreciate your question, I'll be leaving the sequence of the deserting troops being shot as they fled, because that's what happens in war."

Yup. If anyone needed me, I would be under my desk. Permanently. Thinking about the schooling that had just been gracefully delivered to me by the GOAT of moviemaking. Of course he had contemplated the implication of including the sequence in the film. Those are the kinds of things you consider when you have more than forty years of experience as the most commercially successful and critically acclaimed filmmaker of all time. That experience is what affords perspective. The perspective to make bold, creative choices, but even more, the perspective to make wise decisions.

ENTRY-LEVEL ENTREPRENEUR

The beginning of my voyage into the choppy waters of entrepreneurship was hard. After a long career inside big companies running large teams, the transition to a start-up environment with just a handful of people was jarring. Uncomfortable because it was different, but triggering because of how often things seemed to go wrong. There were fires everywhere, every day. Having been in organizations that rarely saw fires, or that had the subject matter experts to extinguish them before they got big, this was a new phenomenon for me.

I'd jumped into this assignment for the challenge. I was excited and nervous for the opportunity to grow doing something new. What I didn't expect was that the frequency of the problems in the business would have me second-guessing my ability to do the work required. I thought these problems were happening because I was unable to predict them, unable to preempt them from happening.

Those early days of scaling drained my confidence and compromised my motivation. I found myself indecisively pulling away from getting my nails dirty. I became a victim of impostor syndrome, worried that I'd be found out for not having the skills to do the work.

Then one day, in the midst of the fires and the insecurity and the frustration of feeling like a failure trying to run a small business, my then-wife, Rachel, was asked to speak at an event that also featured author, speaker, and pastor John Maxwell. As we were backstage with this godfather of leadership sharing the hand-wringing feeling of trying to figure out how to keep problems from happening, he said something that will always stick with me; something to the effect of, "A leader never has two good days in a row. Two days without problems. That's just a fact of running a small business. So, you can decide to either run a small business, or have multiple good days in a row, but you can't have both."

So you're saying problems are normal? Par for the course? To be expected in the journey of building something new? Indeed.

The price of entry for the life you're building is appreciating that it comes with the guarantee that along the way you will face problems you haven't faced before. You will have to navigate through terrain and learn from failure at a rate you've likely not experienced before. But my hope in drawing this to your attention is that it allows you the same sigh of relief I was able to take when John blessed me with the perspective that this was normal. That perspective offered me permission to accept those mistakes as par for the course. It was the conviction from which he delivered that perspective that afforded me the grace to go easy on myself on hard days. The courage to get back up when the next fire knocked me down.

THE VALUE OF EXPERIENCE

John Maxwell is a wise man. His wisdom and perspective are born from years of experience that I didn't have, and won't acquire for some time. The same can be said for my grandmother. My grandma Lee is a baller. She's so wise, sassy, and strong. At nearly a century of life, she's seen it all. So when she called me in the midst of this latest journey of becoming to ask me how it was going, I gave it to her straight as I always do.

I told her, "It's been hard but good. I'm hopeful and terrified. Stronger and still sad."

And that's the thing with moving into the unknown. It requires an ability to hold both at the same time. To know that it makes you normal to be both excited and scared. Encouraged and insecure. The duality is part of what produces growth. That it exists is a sign that you're doing something right in creating distance from your comfort zone.

In the way that only a ninety-nine-year-old can, my grandma told me something that I need to tell you. She said, "Well, David, I can tell you this:

I've been through a lot of hard times. I've experienced so much loss and so much pain, and the thing I know, having been through it, is that I always got to the other side. Every single time. And you will too. You won't enjoy it while it's happening, but the hard parts will always give way to the good."

This woman was the daughter of immigrants, a veteran of war, a single mother to five who made it through divorce, buried another husband, lost a son to cancer and a grandson by suicide, got a front-row seat to the perils of mental illness, and has now said goodbye to nearly all of her friends. As I said, she's been through it all. And in every case, she sits on the other side of the hardest seasons of her life.

Sometimes it takes the perspective of a ninety-nine-year-old rock star to remind you of the fact that you'll see the other side too. Forging into the unknown is not for the faint of heart. You'll face struggle and fear. You'll question your worthiness, but like every headwind that's inevitably going to come your way, this, too, shall pass.

As we begin our journey together, please know that struggle will exist in any new adventure. It will be hard because it's supposed to be. There will be problems along the way. That is the price of entry. But the good news is that you will get through the struggle and the problems and the hard days. Courage is something that you can often cultivate yourself, but at times when the going gets really tough, it's something that you are going to have to borrow from someone who has the gift of perspective that you don't yet possess. Don't take it from me. Take it from my extraordinary grandma Lee; the most prolific filmmaker of all time, Steven Spielberg; and your friend John Maxwell.

LOGBOOK

JOURNALING ACTIVITY

Seek out someone who can give you the gift of perspective in an area of the life you're trying to build. Looking to start a small business? Find someone in your life who has. Or read a book, listen to a podcast, or watch a YouTube video that helps normalize what you're worried about. Considering adoption to complete your family? Set a coffee date with someone in your life who has been through the process, or find a book, podcast, or a YouTube video as a resource that helps frame some of what to expect in the journey. Your courage will come from the proximity you create with people further along a route you're readying yourself to take.

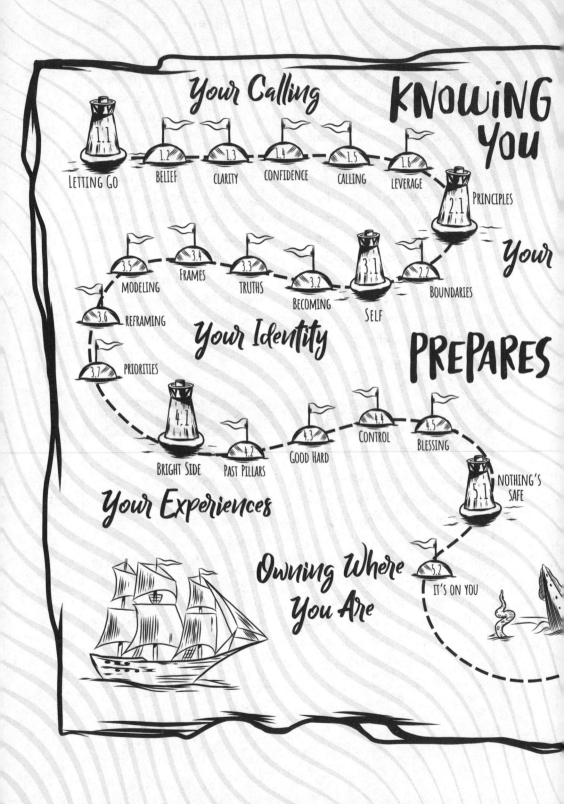

WHERE ARE

YOUR GIFTS

8.8

8.7 GRACE

Values

GROWTH 8.6

8.5 WILLINGNESS

8.4 INTEGRITY

8.3 FLEXIBILITY

8.2 DISCIPLINE

What It's Going To Take

YOU FOR

Faith 8.1

WHERE YOU ARE GOING!

7.6 DEATH IS COMING

PREPARATION 7.5

WORRY 7.4

OTHER PEOPLE 7.3

NEEDS 6.1

FOCUS 6.2

6.3

VISION

6.4 INTENTION

7.1 NAME IT

7.2 EXPOSURE

Building A Plan

Confronting Your Fear

YOUR MAP

NAVIGATING TOWARD COURAGE

THIS BOOK IS structured as a journey. It will become your instruction manual for leaving your safe harbor, navigating the rough waters of fear and uncertainty, and sailing courageously toward a purpose-filled life. The map on the previous pages depict your voyage. As you progress through each chapter, you will encounter buoys that will aid your navigation, helping you to chart your progress and track your journey.

YOU CAN'T SAIL THE OCEAN WITH SOMEONE ELSE'S MAP

So how did I get here? My year of triumph and struggle didn't arrive out of the blue. In many ways, it was a long time coming and the seeds of my journey were sown years ago.

In 2017, as president of distribution at Disney's movie studio, I was on a path that should have made me happy. But despite having been at the helm for the biggest year in movie business history (2016), and being part of the relaunch of the *Star Wars* franchise in 2015, and despite having the title, status, and salary that I thought I'd always wanted, I was unhappy and unfulfilled. The strength of the films, teams, and company leverage left few of my talents necessary to succeed. In a world where I could no longer ignore the call to reclaim the dreams I'd had as a kid to use my unique gifts for telling stories to encourage others, I found myself in a bit of a midlife crisis. After more than twenty years of hard work in the entertainment business, I'd landed on the other side of the ocean, only to realize this destination was not where I wanted to be.

I felt lost. I knew with certainty that it was time to leave my career for my calling, but with no perfect sense of where to head next, I realized in retrospect that I had made a misstep. In the absence of a clear understanding of how to best use my gifts and tap into my passions, I had simply decided to go where someone else was going, to guide my journey using someone else's map.

ON THE WAY TO LOST

During this time of uncertainty, I found myself sitting in the back row of a small auditorium in Austin, Texas, at the first RISE Live Weekend women's conference, which my former wife, Rachel, was hosting. This conference grew out of an idea she'd been working on for years, and it would lead to a larger series of events that would touch the lives of tens of thousands of people who would attend.

Though there were bugs to be worked out, that first event made a massive impact—both on the attendees and on me. The single-day combo platter of inspiration, motivation, and dancing was something you had to be in the room to completely appreciate: an invitation for the nearly two hundred women in attendance to reframe their experiences and believe in themselves in a way they may not have before.

As we walked to lunch during the break that day, I said to Rachel, "I've just seen my future." I could take my experience from entertainment and help her achieve her dreams. She had bottled something unlike anything anyone had ever seen before, and I knew she had a set of superpowers that made her a person who could change people's lives. Desperate for direction, this was the answer I'd been waiting for: a glimpse into the future, this vision of us working together to help build her platform and start a movement.

Our conversation over lunch put the wheels in motion. We flew back home to California after RISE, and before long, we had planned a return trip to Austin to scope it out as a possible place to transplant our family, and her company, to build our future, to chase our dream. I began plotting out how I'd leave Disney, and how we'd transition from everything we'd ever known in California to this new thing in this new place.

Turns out, there was a problem.

It wasn't *our* dream. It was *her* dream.

I'd been happily supporting Rachel's business financially for a decade as she scaled it before the leap, and I had long been her biggest cheerleader. These were things I'd do again in a heartbeat as a husband and best friend. Only now I can see how the decision to pursue this future together came at a time when my judgment was compromised. My vision was impaired. My midlife moment had disabled my ability to tap into my own imagination. So I borrowed someone else's.

And yes, in that first eighteen months of adventure we went on to build something at The Hollis Company that in its attempts to put resources in people's lives through books, podcasts, coaching, live events, and products still makes me so proud, and that I know has had an incredible impact on so many. And yes, I'll root for Rachel and that team for the rest of time, even as our relationship has changed, as she has evolved and even as I've transitioned out of the business to do work of my own. You see, it wasn't until I was in our business that I was able to see that it was *her* business and her vision, not ours. It took me some time to realize that I needed to find a way to tap into *my* passions, talents, and abilities to bring light to the world. I needed a map of my own.

A CALLING FROM THE PAST

As I was grappling with all of this, I had an experience that can only be described as divine intervention. I was serendipitously seated on a plane next to my childhood hero, Dan Rather. I was and am a nerd, leave me be.

He couldn't have been a nicer person: generous with his conversation about the current state of media and sharing many insights from his life and career. We also discussed ways to find optimism when the world feels scary, which was incredibly reassuring coming from one of the most trusted people on the planet.

What Mr. Rather couldn't have known was the way our encounter reminded me of my dreams as a nineteen-year-old communications major. How the local news desk I anchored in Southern California or the vaunted 2:00 a.m. slot as a deejay on the college radio station brought me so much joy, and helped paint a picture for me of whom I thought I'd become when I grew up.

Back then, I thought I'd become Dan Rather.

Our conversation on that flight unlocked something in me. I was lost in that moment, and I needed to be reminded of what my dreams had been as a nineteen-year-old in order to forge a vision of my future. I had to reconnect with the kid inside who believed that anything was possible. I had to get back in touch with my passion for media and reporting. It had never gone away, but had just been dormant. Today, I might not be hosting the evening news like Dan Rather. But writing books, hosting a podcast, creating social media content, and serving as a coach through my digital offerings are all forms of reporting. I am taking the things I'm good at and combining those with my area of passion.

That moment of clarity on the plane with Dan Rather arrived after years of fighting the tide. If you've made the same misstep that I did of mistaking someone else's dreams for your own, rest assured: all hope is not lost. These choices were part of a larger map that happened to include a fortuitous detour. The skills developed, relationships forged, and lessons learned are all still crucial markers, buoys if you will, lining the route that leads to your ultimate destination. These "mistakes" have gifted you with the experience needed to embark on the next leg of your journey. This is the leg where you choose the destination and set the course.

In my case, following Rachel's dream brought me closer to mine. Like following a map from the United States to Australia, only to realize you were meant to be in New Zealand, it took crossing the ocean, losing sight of the shore, and ultimately realizing that I was landing at the wrong destination to see how relatively close I was to mine.

I don't want you to wait until your version of Dan Rather sits down next to you on a plane to acknowledge what you already know: in the work to uncover your calling, make sure you're playing the role of captain.

LOGBOOK

JOURNALING ACTIVITY

Grab a notebook or a journal and consider the following questions. Then jot down your responses. As you continue on this journey, you will find it helpful to return to your answers from time to time.

- What did you want to be before you became who you are?
- What did the nineteen-year-old version of you dream about?
- What were your sources of joy before you had your current life responsibilities and obligations?

SECTION 1
WHERE YOU ARE

YOUR
CALLING

As we begin this journey together, we'll spend this first section of the book understanding *where you are*. You see, you can't put together the plan for where you are going or what it will take to get there if you don't know where you're starting from. For the purposes of our voyage together in this book, let's refer to where you are currently as the harbor, where you sit safely anchored and tied to the dock. This represents your attachment to the experiences of your past and the identity you've come to assume over time.

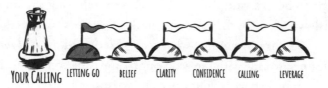

YOUR CALLING LETTING GO BELIEF CLARITY CONFIDENCE CALLING LEVERAGE

THE THING ABOUT THE HARBOR

The anonymous quote "You'll never cross the ocean unless you lose sight of the shore" comes into play here. To begin, we need to accept the idea that in order to end up where we want to be, we have to let go of where we've been. Lose sight of the shore. Let go of the harbor.

Easier said than done. All of us humans live in a harbor that was either built for us:

- By other people such as our family of origin, societal norms, or religious beliefs.
- Through the lens of the roles we've played, such as partner, parent, or executive.
- Through the way we've assigned positive and negative value to the experiences of our past.

Or some combination of all three.

Leaving what you know for what you need is scary. There is comfort in the familiar, even if it is not serving you. We cling to the stories we have been told about who we are and what our lives should be. We feel safe inhabiting the often limiting roles that we've inherited from our families, from society, and from our past. The trouble is, these preordained roles are often holding us back from where we want to go, and who we're here to be.

So, as we prepare to set sail, we're faced with some tough choices. Are we willing to let go of the things that are weighing us down in order to cross the ocean? Can we make peace with what we'll leave behind? Can we accept that our decision to set off for new shores may make certain people in our lives uncomfortable?

These are difficult choices. But the only way to become not just who you want to be but who you *need* to be is by rejecting the limitations handed down to you by society, your family of origin, your experiences, or your expectations surrounding what *good girls* do or how *real men* show up. It's time to wrestle with the way your past may be compromising your present. It's time to rewrite your story, and to stop telling yourself that you aren't ready or capable enough to face the voyage ahead. It's time.

In doing so, you'll be given the opportunity to leave behind the pieces of who you've been, what you've believed, and how you've behaved that don't serve what sits on the other side of this journey. The new, more whole, closer-to-fulfilled version of you on the other side of the ocean requires first that you make peace with leaving the harbor. Let go of where you are for where you're headed. Anchors up.

LOGBOOK

JOURNALING ACTIVITY

In the following exercise, I want you to take stock of where you are today, consider the following questions, and write out your answers.

- Why haven't you already left your safe harbor?
- What are the internal and external forces that are keeping you confined to your comfort zone?
- What "ropes" from your past are currently keeping you tied to the dock?
- Has suffering become part of your identity in a way that makes trying to move away from it scary?
- Do you believe you deserve something better than what you currently experience every day?

SAILBOATS AND WIND

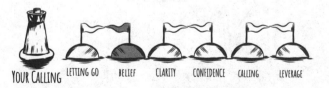

YOUR CALLING   LETTING GO   BELIEF   CLARITY   CONFIDENCE   CALLING   LEVERAGE

Do you think you can be the man you were meant to be while married to me?

In the midst of what was supposed to have been my best year ever, the floor fell out from under me as my then wife asked me this question. It was the beginning of our end. In the span of eight minutes, the identity that I'd clung to most closely, that of her husband, went from clear to blurry.

Getting a divorce, a previously unthinkable and unexpected life event, took what had been a clear sense of who I was and where I was headed and turned it on its head. My ex-wife and I were not only life partners, but we were in business together, which made things especially complicated. The question of who I was, both personally and professionally, when our marriage ended, shattered my vision for the future and left me needing to imagine something new altogether. It turns out that's what happens when you make plans and life has different designs. I know I'm not alone in this experience.

I spent a year weathering the storms of identity shift, grieving what was. I confronted the terrifying and exhilarating experience of staring at a blank canvas and deciding what my new life would look like. During this turbulent period, I would often sit out on my back patio listening to music to calm my anxiety. Music became my way of manufacturing peace and maintaining focus when the storm surrounding me felt disorienting and overwhelming.

I dubbed this sacred space my "patio of peace." Among the many inspirations was a singer-songwriter named Ben Rector whose songs felt like they had been written specifically for my trek into the unknown. On highest rotation was Ben's song "Sailboat," in which feelings of despair and hope are held in equal weight over the course of just a few chords. The lyrics mirrored my feeling of having been pushed out to sea, lost from what I knew, waiting for some kind of wind to blow me back home. Back to something that felt normal again.

I feel just like a sailboat
I don't know where I'm headed
But you can't make the wind blow
From a sailboat

I've listened to this song 4,241 times, and have cried every single time it came on. Tears of grief for what had been. Tears over giving up on the illusion of control. Tears of hope for what could be. The promise of the next shore. The promise of finding a new purpose.

But I'm not giving up
I'm gonna move on forward
I'm gonna raise my sail
God knows what I'm headed towards

I never lost faith that I would find that new purpose and reach the next shore. But I had to accept that I wouldn't be able to control the timing, or the conditions. Turns out that's how faith works. Faith is knowing you'll get there, even if you don't know how or when.

Only change I see
Lost or found at sea
The only difference
Is believing I'll make it in

Whatever storm you are weathering, be it relationship change, the loss of a loved one, a professional challenge, or the general funk of a life that ought to feel like more than it does, keep the faith. The lost are found at sea. You will make it to the next shore. So we start this journey with a promise that this season is building something in us that we may never have known we had: the courage to make it back in. The choppy waters of these unfamiliar waves enable us to emerge new, different, better, and stronger when we hit the land on the other side.

If you're feeling despair today, lost at sea in an unrecognizable world, find the courage to raise your sail. It may seem impossible at first, but it's my hope for you that in this book you will tap into a power far greater than your fear that already knows what you're headed for.

As much as this book will dive into how to get to where you're heading, one of the first and most important acts is *belief*. Believing you will make it. Cultivating the courage to believe that you deserve something more, that you are resilient enough to keep going when it gets hard. You will only become who you aspire to be by facing the fears that inevitably come up along the way.

And even if you are not feeling fear now, I want to prepare you for the fact that you will at some point in this journey. Pushing into new spaces invites your insecurities in a way that will find you at times floating and waiting for wind, and at other times disoriented by the raging storm.

The thing you need to keep sight of today, and any day when those feelings emerge, is the guarantee that you will ultimately find your new self. You will reach the shore on the other side. It is there. It will always be there. And you will get there, not in spite of the conditions you have to travel through, but because of them.

LOGBOOK

JOURNALING ACTIVITY

Make a list of every hard thing you have been through in your life to this point and how you overcame those challenges. Read over your list, remember how you felt when you faced that storm and when you overcame it, then draw confidence from your past successes, and open yourself up to the work that is needed to rise in this moment. You have been lost at sea before. Reconnect with your ability to stay strong, to be patient, and to practice resilience. These abilities grow stronger each time you are tested.

SEEKING STILLNESS

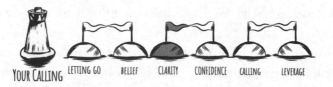

YOUR CALLING   LETTING GO   BELIEF   CLARITY   CONFIDENCE   CALLING   LEVERAGE

The fast-paced modern world is often at odds with an essential ingredient required for connecting with our inner selves and our desires: stillness. As a result, we must be intentional about slowing down and making the time to rest, reflect, and dream. Engineer quiet moments. Cultivate calm. There are various ways of doing this. Some of us choose meditation, some a hot bath, others time in nature or the solitude that comes in a long run.

In late 2019, to find the next-level stillness I needed to manufacture my ambitious best year ever, I traveled to a place in the desert outside of Tucson, Arizona, where for three days I sat on a rock. Alone. Open notebook. No technology. No agenda. Well, okay, there was a small agenda. I was on a mission to find my purpose. Little thing. As previously described, I felt unmoored.

As I drove to the airport, an Avicii song came on and I started to cry. Out of nowhere. I mean, I like this guy's music, but this was about something else. On an assignment to find myself, I worried that I might come back having discovered that there wasn't anything to find. Maybe I would sit in nature for three days only to discover that happiness and fulfillment were things reserved for other people but not available to me.

Maybe I had been so consumed by the identities of husband and father that I no longer knew who I was. A special blend of people pleasing, co-dependence, and a desire to be loved had me familiar with acquiescing to the needs and interests of my closest people so much that I was unable to answer the simple question "What do you like to do in your spare time?" I'd spent so much time trying to be (and often failing completely to be) who my partner and kids, or parents, or my church, or society wanted me to be that I lost sight of who I wanted to be. Who I was meant to be. Couldn't even tell you what I liked. I'd lost touch with my true desires and my passions. Anyone relate?

When I ventured into the desert, I had recently finished reading a book by Ryan Holiday called *Stillness Is the Key*, and I challenged myself to see what popped up when I did as his book recommended and made stillness an intention.

In testing his hypothesis that any season of chaos or crisis you find yourself in can be better navigated by slowing down and tuning out the noise, it turned out to be a powerful experience and one that I can't recommend enough. So I sat out there in the desert and scribbled my thoughts in a small green notebook with a ship scrawled on its front. My first entry read, "Well, I'm writing in a journal. How exciting." Then I drew a straight-faced emoji. The notion of being alone, of giving myself permission to take time away from my family and work, felt strange. The idea of doing this without a detailed agenda felt even stranger.

By filling up a notebook with things I didn't even know I was thinking, I was able to have the breakthroughs that were needed to create the kind of life I wanted in the coming year. In that notebook, I cast a specific, detailed vision for how I wanted to emerge on the other side. Thirty-eight single-lined pages describing how I'd tend to my health and my mindset, cater to my personal passions, invest in my faith, and draw closer to my most important relationships. I even included the most intricate nuances

of how I'd dress, carry myself, and feel when I looked in the mirror. The detailed inventory of the life I wanted came complete with insights into how I'd have to show up if I actually wanted the life I'd been writing about.

Never having journaled before, I had no idea how powerful this practice could be. I wrote in my green notebook for three days, almost without stopping. When I'd start each journaling session, the first twenty minutes or so were a warm-up to get out the things sitting at the top of my consciousness, thoughts I already knew I'd had, the stuff I needed to do, details that were causing stress and anxiety for me that I was already well aware of. But then, after the twenty-minute mark, something magical would happen. I'd write things that I wasn't even aware I'd been thinking. Now I was tapping into my subconscious where I'd been pushing down feelings and storing my unprocessed emotions. By deleting social media from my phone, carving out this time, and setting an intention with stillness, I was finally able to see and hear what I hadn't been able to in the busy day-to-day of "normal" life.

Before I left the desert, I had a vision for the life I wanted going forward. While some of the details still needed polishing, I knew I wanted to tackle a massive physical challenge in my first marathon, but still needed to train. I knew that I wanted to craft a career out of writing and speaking, of making an impact through the tools I create, but hadn't yet fully stepped out from behind the scenes. As much as MrDaveHollis.com might become a destination for these tools, I wasn't yet a published author, coach, or podcast host. I'd only just begun to speak on stages. Most of this was still just an unrelenting tug from my intuition. I didn't have all the answers, but I did have direction.

Using what I discovered in the desert, I began to approach my search for purpose in an entirely new way. My morning routine now included space for silence, journaling, and meditation. I still went for my usual long runs and bike rides, but I intermittently went without the music that had always fueled me, allowing myself to be with my thoughts. My back patio, the every-evening destination to slow down and listen to my emotions from the day.

It turns out that stillness isn't just a valuable resource for getting clarity on where you are. It's also important for maintaining sanity once you've committed to ditching the harbor. Deciding to move away from your familiar will introduce chaos in your life, and that chaos will take you under unless you have a way of regaining equilibrium.

The storms you encounter at sea will initially leave you wanting to cut your journey short and return to shore. Slowing down, getting patient, and creating space to process what you're experiencing is the only way you'll be able to make it through. Only in the calm, away from the chaos, can you nurture the courage you'll need for the journey.

The stillness I experienced during my three days in the desert gave me clarity once I returned. I had answers to the question of where I was headed. I could clearly see the connection between who I hoped to be and the kind of work I'd need to do every day to get there. This is something I'll discuss further in the *Linear Journey Ahead* section, as we dive into an exercise I call "If/Then," as in *if* I want this kind of life, *then* I need to do these kinds of things to get there.

Slowing down and stepping away from my regularly scheduled programming during my time in the desert made me question whether that programming should even exist at all. It made me consider what mattered and what didn't.

You don't need a desert. It may be a patio chair, closet floor, yoga mat, or parked car that does the trick. You don't need three days. It may be thirty minutes before the kids get up or a two-hour self-care Saturday each month.

You do, however, need to fight to create intentionally still moments. The world around you runs on noise. Never-ending marketing from companies trying to convince you of what you desperately need. The news business betting that they can keep you just scared enough to keep tuning in. Social media's comparison trap that has you triggered hourly by how your real life stacks up to the curated highlight reels of the people you follow. That noise creates a chaos that will never allow you to get to the bottom of what actually matters. That incessant clamor drowns out your ability to focus on how you become who you were meant to be.

So turn down the volume. Intentionally create time in silence, in a slowed pace to allow yourself the ability to see where you're going.

And wouldn't you know it, when I returned from the desert, not only did I have a clear vision for the life I wanted to live and what it would take to get there, but I was also able to make that list of the things I like to do in my spare time. I'm a nerd for sports memorabilia. Actually enjoy running. Am carving out time to learn how to play the guitar, a thing I always wanted to do. A seemingly small assignment that led to so many interesting break-throughs about where my passions lie in my search for "why." Praise be.

THE HUBRIS OF A TWENTY-THREE-YEAR-OLD

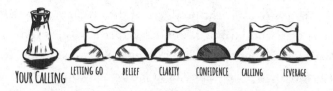

YOUR CALLING LETTING GO BELIEF CLARITY CONFIDENCE CALLING LEVERAGE

I love sports. Always have. Baseball, football, basketball; frankly, anything with a ball, I'm in. It's at the core of my being.

Half a lifetime ago, when I was twenty-three and working one of my first jobs out of college as a coordinator in Twentieth Century Fox's pub-licity department, the Super Bowl was being played in Miami. At the time, I was making $22,400 a year and eating the wildly underrated chicken-flavored Top Ramen four nights a week to afford my LA apartment. More than anything on earth, I wanted to work the game that Fox was broad-casting that year.

I was young, inexperienced, and had little to offer the show producers, but I went to management anyway and asked if there was a way for me to be part of the event. I made my best case. They said no, explaining that it wasn't in the budget to send me out there and that they hoped I under-stood. They appreciated my passion, but it was a hard no. Their point of view was difficult to argue with. On paper it made sense, given my lack of experience. So I did what any cocky twenty-three-year-old would do. I marched back into my boss's boss's boss's office with a copy of a plane ticket to Miami that I had bought for myself and suggested that I was willing to do literally anything that might help.

Of course, that ticket was way more than I could afford, and buying it meant that ramen would be on the menu seven nights a week for a bit. But it felt like a smart trade-off at this point in my life. I also convinced my best pal, Paul, who was actually working at the event, to let me sleep on the couch in his hotel room. I knew I could be of value to the company down in Miami even if they couldn't see it. I heard the reason they couldn't have me: "It's not in our budget." And I eliminated it.

And my boss's boss's boss, a guy named George, said yes. Shaking his head, he agreed to a thing that didn't make conventional sense because he was impressed with my initiative and my willingness to do whatever it took to get there. I'd found a way to overcome my lack of experience.

I was assigned to assist the producer of the pregame show, a grizzled industry veteran who'd worked countless Super Bowls. As you can imagine, when he found out that I'd be working the show with him, he was as excited as you could imagine he'd be at having someone on his team who had no experience. Not excited. When I arrived on-site, he gave me a mission: get a Hall of Fame coach from a makeup chair to the broadcast booth. Point A to point B. "So, you're saying I have one job?" I asked him. "I can do this job. Thank you very much."

Eventually this coach, whom I had watched and revered my entire life, whose name even the non-sports fan might know, was ready to be moved and I was eager to kill my assignment. We were just a few steps out of my producer's earshot when the coach said to me, "Kid, we gotta make a quick pit stop." He told me that he had four field passes that he couldn't use and that we had to run out to the parking lot to find a scalper. Ummm. This was not on my itinerary. I barely got here. I had no idea what to do.

I was the kid who didn't toilet paper houses. Rather, I was the "lookout" safely down the street. I got good grades, had a wild time at Youth Group, and stayed out of trouble (usually for not having been invited near it). I can still feel the knots in my stomach at that moment. He might as well have offered me crack.

I was terrified of screwing up my new job. I did my best to explain to him that his detour wasn't possible. We didn't have time. We didn't have approval. I'd committed to ramen to be here. He put his hand on my shoulder, nodded, and very confidently said, "I'll take it from here."

He was not worried. This wasn't his first rodeo. I assumed my familiar role as lookout as he went out to the parking lot to sell the tickets for

$10,000. It took four minutes. I felt like I was in *GoodFellas*. Once our little adventure was over, we made it to the booth. Just as planned. Just as I had been asked to do. And as we said our goodbyes, he slipped me $500 for being a trusty accomplice. Back to ramen for just four nights a week.

Not long after returning to Los Angeles, my initiative was rewarded. I'd been working on a show called *The X-Files*. When a decision to take the show on a nationwide tour came up, they asked if I would consider taking on the role of "talent wrangler." In addition to my Monday through Friday responsibilities, I jumped at the chance to fly with the cast each weekend to old blimp hangars and creepy abandoned buildings that fit the show's otherworldly aesthetic.

The success of that tour helped me land my next job at a public relations and talent management agency where I took on a roster of personalities like Ricki Lake and Melissa Joan Hart, and corporate clients like *Sports Illustrated*. The experience provided extraordinary growth and a broadening of my set of skills. In many ways it all came back to my unapologetic advocacy for myself and the creativity required to turn a no into a yes.

By sharing this story I don't mean to suggest for a second that your journey into the unknown should veer into crimes and misdemeanors. But I do think that many of us, myself included, would do well to reconnect with some of the hubris and ambition of our twenty-three-year-old selves (and if you weren't as confident or driven as I was, you may borrow some of mine; there was plenty to go around). Channel that willingness to do whatever it took to turn a no into a yes in life. Roll with the punches that an unfamiliar journey may throw your way. Connect to the courage you had before the world sold you fear and you accepted it at face value.

When I think of that Miami Super Bowl experience, it brings me back to a point in my life when I pursued my dreams like I had nothing to lose, when I didn't know enough to accept "no," when I didn't have reservations about chasing who I was trying to become. I was 100 percent driven by my passion for broadcast television and sports, willing to look like a fool, and even prepared to forgo a short-term balanced diet to reach my goals. On the days when I get nervous about what's next, I try to reconnect to this younger, dumber but braver, more confident version of me.

The guy who bought a plane ticket he couldn't afford to advance his career. The guy who went along for a ride because it was part of what it took to get the job done.

This decision to leave your safe harbor and pursue your dream will require you to make some uncomfortable moves. You will have to face your uncertainty and push past your fear. So channel the ambition of that twentysomething version of yourself who would have done what it took to stand on the field while Cher belted out the National Anthem, or whatever your equivalent of going to the Super Bowl might be. Have the courage to manufacture opportunity when other people try to tell you what you can't do. Push back against the fear of being rejected. Acclimate to the uncertainty you'll inevitably face. It will be well worth it.

LOGBOOK

JOURNALING ACTIVITY

Write a letter to yourself from your younger self who was full of dreams, believed in endless possibilities, wasn't as afraid, and had more confidence (even if it wasn't yet supported by experience). What would that dreamer tell you? How might that young person encourage you to believe again as you did then?

WHAT WOULD YOU HAVE ME ACCOMPLISH?

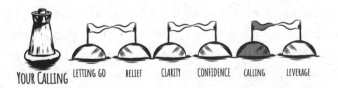

YOUR CALLING LETTING GO BELIEF CLARITY CONFIDENCE CALLING LEVERAGE

None of us consciously chooses to stay in our suffering. But fear of the unknown often causes us to rationalize staying stuck in the familiar, even when it's not serving us. We opt for what we know, being okay with just being okay, over the freedom that sits on the other side of our fear.

Layer on top the way we worry about what other people will think of us as we're getting our sea legs in this new adventure. How easy is it to convince ourselves that we'll make our move when we can do it without publicly failing, or when we can do it in a way that will not inconvenience *them*, or when we feel like we have *their* permission, or when we find a way to do it and still be deemed acceptable by *their* standards.

When never comes. Your fear will always exist. Their opinions will never go away. You're faced with the tough choice of either casting off or denying your true self, talking yourself out of your dreams, quieting your intuition, and ignoring that you may have been placed here for a reason in the attempt to keep others happy and avoid facing your fear.

At what costs? At the expense of your fulfillment, your freedom. At the expense of feeling proud of yourself. At the expense of your kids having someone they'd do anything to become. At the expense of the legacy you could have had. At the expense of intimacy, of anyone ever getting to know you. The real you.

So often, the person who finds themselves stuck is asking, "What would you have me accomplish?" to the wrong audience. They're asking the opinions of other people. They're asking the doubt and fear of their own insecurities. They're asking the hard things they've been through in their past. They're asking the antiquated programming from their family of origin, the societal norms offering how to play it safe and be deemed "good."

None of these are the audience for that question. None. Catering to what they would have you accomplish will only leave you unquenched, longing for more, as the not-quite-proud, partial version of yourself, denying the intention of the only audience worthy of the question.

How do we gain the confidence needed to take this leap? How do we give ourselves permission to leave the harbor? As we close this section of the book, the answer comes in understanding how you might honor the intention of your creator.

Our deepest feelings of happiness come when we can fulfill the measure of our creation.

You were created for a reason. Deliberate, meticulous design. Of the billions of people on this planet, of the billions more who've ever lived, you are the only one ever created as you. The way your brain works, the things that you're great at, the way you experience all your feelings and everything that you've been through, they are all exclusive to you. A limited edition. One of one. And in this deliberate design, an intention was cast for how you, and only you, might wield these gifts.

What would it mean to fully unlock the gifts intended for this world by becoming who you were placed here to be? What would it mean to accept that you were made this way on purpose? How might you feel compelled to pursue your dreams if you believed with every part of your being that those dreams were intentionally gifted to you by a creator who hoped you'd act on them?

Each of us is created with a unique set of talents. Each of us is given the gift of a distinct set of experiences on this planet. That gift comes with the mandate to share our skills and wisdom with the world. If the nature of this voyage overwhelms you, can you find permission, even motivation, in knowing that it was ordained by a power beyond your own? Intentionally. By design.

When I was at a low point, stuck, overwhelmed by fear, and unsure of myself and my ability to step off the dock and into the ship that would take me into the unknown in the aftermath of divorce, my friend Ethan Willis said something that allowed me to cultivate the courage to keep going: "Fulfillment and power will flow through us when we recognize that we are part of something greater and tap into a capacity beyond our own."

That capacity beyond our own comes from a higher power. For me, it's a God I believe in as a Christian. For you, be it my God or not, my conversation with Ethan boiled it down to asking two important questions of our higher power:

- What did my creator specifically design me to do?
- What would it mean to shift the plea from "help me accomplish these goals" to "what would you have me accomplish"?

Our talents and life experiences are our passport, our mandate to do the things we feel called to achieve. Embrace your calling. Surrender to it. Ask, "What would you have me accomplish?" And when the answer comes in the form of the unrelenting whisper of your intuition to do something that scares you, the way your heart races when you dream so big you're bound to fail along the way, the way your gut instinct draws you in a certain direction that you're just not yet totally prepared for, or doors open for something you just know you have to do even though you don't know how you'll do it . . . step off the dock. Step onto the ship. Sail toward your fear, through the opinions of other people, over the waves of dogmatic thinking, against the current of societal programming. To freedom. To becoming who you were meant to be.

You were made this way. On purpose. You can't fail as you fulfill the measure of your creation.

Looking for permission to come aboard? Permission granted. Let's go.

LOGBOOK

JOURNALING ACTIVITY

In the back of your notebook or journal, bookmark a page, and at the top, write out the question "What Would You Have Me Accomplish?" As you work your way through this book, every time you get a clue, hear a whisper from your intuition, or feel a sign present itself, open to your bookmarked page and add it to your running list. This isn't a question answered quickly, but it's also a question that's never answered if we don't ask it.

WHY, OH WHY?

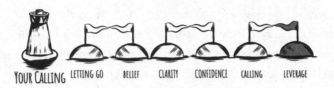

YOUR CALLING · LETTING GO · BELIEF · CLARITY · CONFIDENCE · CALLING · LEVERAGE

Can I quickly address one of the biggest ways that you're going to sabotage your progress before we even begin? You're not going to want me to do it, but I've got to. Here it is: making excuses.

Excuses for not maintaining healthy habits, for not sticking to a morning routine, for not moving your body enough, for not getting to bed early, for not asking for help when you need it, for watching TV instead of reading, for saying yes when you need to say no. Stop making excuses for why you are not currently doing the things required to unlock the possibility of the life you say you want. You'll either tilt the odds in your favor by intentionally engineering the kind of life you deserve through the commitments that come with it . . . or you won't.

Hard work alone doesn't guarantee the life of your dreams, but a lack of discipline eliminates any possibility of even getting close. You gotta connect to a "why" that's stronger than your excuses.

My "why" starts with honoring the intention of my creator. Believing that I was placed on this planet with deliberate design and the responsibility for action that comes in having been endowed with so much potential. My "why" is about how I hope to feel about myself when I'm by myself and know I've given my best effort. It's the drive to show up for the life I believe I was built for and deserve. It's the model I aspire to be for my children, acting like the kind of adult I hope they each become. It's the impact I seek to afford others as a tribute to the unique talents I've been given.

And, as you'll see in the *Finding Your Why* section at the end of the book, your "why" is also about the intersection of:

- Passion. It sets your heart on fire.
- Mastery. It's something you're great at.

- Impact. It brings needed light to the world.
- Sustenance. It can create financial security for you.

Now, if you struggle to know what your "why" is or don't have one currently that's stronger than staying stuck, do not panic. As I mentioned, we finish this book with a deep dive into how you find your "why," what may be keeping you from connecting to it, and how to access it as leverage to keep you focused and motivated.

The reality is that we rarely feel like doing hard things. I definitely didn't feel like waking up this morning while it was still dark and going out to my garage gym to work out. But I did it anyway, because doing something physically challenging first thing in the morning helps set the intention for my day, makes me feel strong, and keeps me believing I can handle whatever the day ahead holds. Pushing myself to exercise every morning, even when I feel like making excuses, unlocks how I hope to show up for my kids, my friends, my team, and myself.

I have this written on my bathroom mirror. Bottom right-hand corner for the days I start to reach for an excuse. It's a reminder that the life I aspire to live means doing the things that help me get there, even on the days I don't feel like it:

Don't feel motivated?

Awesome. Me either.

Who cares? Do it anyway.

I say it out loud, laugh at how ridiculous it sometimes feels, and then I get my stupid running shoes on. And you know what will happen once you stop making excuses for why you're not currently doing all of these hard, good things, and you just *do them*? You are going to feel a deep sense of pride and satisfaction for making and honoring commitments to yourself. So, are you willing to step outside of your comfort zone? Are you willing to show up on the days you don't feel like it? What are you willing to sacrifice in order to feel proud of yourself?

Once you're able to generate that pride, you'll also foster the courage necessary to get back up when life throws a curve. The sense of satisfaction

DON'T FEEL MOTIVATED?
AWESOME. ME EITHER.
WHO CARES? DO IT ANYWAY.

you'll feel when you keep the commitments you've made to yourself is a momentum-building motivation hack that will allow you to keep going when others have long given up. Find yourself a "why" that matters more than your excuses, and there's no limit to what you can achieve.

LOGBOOK

JOURNALING ACTIVITY

Think back to a time when you remember being proud of something you'd accomplished. In your journal, detail what that felt like. How did you carry yourself? How did your feeling of accomplishment affect other areas of your life? Can you see the connection between feeling proud and feeling courageous?

YOUR
VALUES

A ncient seafarers plotted their course by the stars. Yes, they used geometry and special instruments and called on the powers of Dwayne "The Rock" Johnson from *Moana*, but for the most part they depended on astronomy to guide their navigation. Finding that North Star kept them moving in the right direction, regardless of the conditions at sea.

SHIP KILLERS

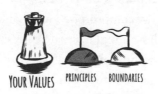

YOUR VALUES   PRINCIPLES   BOUNDARIES

As time went on, maps were developed. Early nautical maps depicted danger symbols known as "ship killers" that marked the location of hazards such as rocks, islets, breakers, reefs, wrecks, obstructions, and spoil areas, helping sailors to avoid running into trouble. These warnings served as the sailors' guiding principles at sea, in much the same way that our core values serve as the guiding principles in our lives. Core values help us to keep track of what we stand for. They act as our guardrails when we run up against trouble, so that we don't run aground. Having a clear sense of what you stand for and making sure that your everyday behavior is in line with your values is an important next piece of the next stage of this book. You see, now that you are a step closer to finding your calling, the next question is: "Who do you need to be consistently over time to allow that calling to come to life?"

I have identified six core values that I want to strive for in my life:

- **Centeredness**—I work to live; I don't live to work.
- **Advocacy**—I will show up as an ally to all, particularly anyone marginalized by the systems and structures that create headwinds I might not experience because of my privilege.
- **Growth**—I will strive to be better today than I was yesterday.
- **Optimism**—I choose positivity; hope in what's to come, the good that can exist even in the hard.
- **Service**—I want to be a servant leader in every aspect of life.
- **Responsibility**—I will endeavor to act with integrity.

These are the traits I hope to exemplify every day. I've signaled to my accountability partners to be on the lookout for them in case I veer off course. I know that if my work starts to compromise my ability to show up as a dad, if negativity in hard times starts painting a pessimistic vision of my future, or one of countless other things begins to fall outside the bounds of these values I've compromised my chances at reaching my goals and have undermined how I might actualize my calling.

Your core values may not look like mine. That's okay. To start the discovery process that led me to defining the six core values I am building my life around, I asked myself the following questions:

- What are the things I'd need to value most to honor my purpose on this planet? How do these beliefs unlock an ability to create integrity between my daily actions and my intentional design?

- How do I want the people I love and respect to describe me? If my behavior were aligned with my values and these important people were to audit my life for thirty days in a row, how would they characterize me? I think of this as the "personal brand" I want to embody. How would someone I love describe it?
- To live in accordance with the "personal brand" to which I aspire, what daily habits and routines do I need to adopt? Will adopting these habits take me closer to my calling? How do the commitments on my calendar align with this vision? How do the people I spend time with support this vision?
- When I live by these values every single day, how do I feel about myself? Is my answer to this question "proud"? If it's not, I need to reevaluate.

DEVELOPING PERSONAL VALUES

WHO DO YOU HOPE TO BE? | WHAT WOULD YOU HAVE TO DO? | HOW DO THESE ACTIONS SUPPORT YOUR GOALS? | HOW WILL YOU FEEL LIVING THESE VALUES?

When I think about why I'm on this planet, I know that my six core values will support that calling. By identifying these values, I am making it my mission to keep my family a priority, to advocate for others, to chase growth, to see the good, to serve well, and to do so in a way that creates consistency between my ambition and my actions. If I drift away from my core values, I risk running into "ship killers" that slow down or even sink my vessel. When I live them fully, I know that I am the most confident, courageous version of myself, sailing toward who I hope to become.

It all starts with the answer to the question: *What do you stand for?* In the coming chapter, we're going to dive into how to build the habits to create the consistency you need to make these values come to life. But unless you know your core values, you won't know what habits and routines to build. Locate that North Star. Create the guardrails that will reinforce what you do and don't do. Be clear about who you hope to show up as every day. As you assume the helm of your ship, you'll give yourself a chance to be that person.

LOGBOOK

JOURNALING ACTIVITY

Now we are going to determine your core values, based on the questions I asked myself to determine mine. In your journal, begin by asking yourself, "What do I stand for?" Then continue on to the following questions, and jot down your four to six core values as you go.

- What are the things I need to value to honor my purpose on this planet?
- How do I want the people I love and respect to describe me? What is the "personal brand" I want to embody?
- In order to live in accordance with my "personal brand," what daily habits and routines do I need to adopt? Will adopting these habits take me closer to my calling?
- If I were to live by these values every single day, how would I feel about myself? Is my answer "proud"?

SHOOTING A HOSTAGE

YOUR VALUES   PRINCIPLES   BOUNDARIES

Six years after Disney's 2009 $4 billion acquisition of Marvel Entertainment, senior leadership began looking for the company's divisions to begin recouping the investment. At the time there was no way of knowing that over the deal's first decade the acquisition would go on to make Disney nearly $20 billion in box office revenue. As is the case in transactions like this, the way to offset the investment was by pushing our partners in every sector to renegotiate their deals with Disney.

As the person responsible for bartering with movie theater owners around the world, it was on me and my team to engage in tough conversations about the price of the upcoming Avengers film. In the movie business, every dollar of a movie ticket is split between the producer of the film (in this case Disney) and the movie theaters, and that split was something that created quite the contentious back-and-forth.

In preparation for the negotiations, we tried to put a value on the acquisition's incremental benefit to theaters. We took into consideration the acquisition cost, the scale of the marketing, and the scope of the production capital in the film slate that in the coming years was expected to drive people into seats. We landed on numbers that we believed were fair, relative to the effort and investment on our side. Of course, we acknowledged that our definition of "fair" was likely to be challenged by the other side.

As expected, the price hike created a fight. The tense negotiations included threats from movie theaters to refuse to play movies at the prices we were coming to the table with. What would be weeks of negotiating in some seventy-five countries required us to walk into the conversations knowing what we believed our value was and defining the line under which we were unwilling to go.

At the time, Marvel was run by an Israeli American businessperson named Ike Perlmutter. A fierce competitor known for driving a hard bargain, Ike was someone with whom I developed a close relationship and from whom I learned a lot. In this instance, he taught me the value of knowing what you stand for, and the power of fighting for it without capitulating under pressure.

Your value is worth what you believe it is if you're willing to walk away from people who can't see it.

He showed me the power of standing your ground, even if it means having to "shoot a hostage" to show how serious you are about your position in the standoff.

It's not that he said those exact words, and no, the theaters weren't being held hostage by any means. Considering the size of these films, they stood to have their biggest paydays of the year. So we decided that if someone threatened not to play the film, we would call their bluff. It would be worth it for Disney if every other theater saw how serious we were. And sure enough, a theater group in Germany decided not to play the film. As we had hoped, the publicity of our unwillingness to undervalue ourselves to meet the demands of those who didn't see our worth sent a clear message to the thousands of other theater operators around the world: we were serious.

The film went on to make more than $1.4 billion worldwide, making it one of the ten biggest films of all time. It proved to be worth the value we'd assigned it, earning a lot of money for both sides and driving millions of people into theaters.

So, what does this have to do with you?

Like the lesson I took from Ike, it's time to stop negotiating your worth with the people who might question it. The ambition you have to grow and evolve, to sail beyond the harbor, will not be one that stays afloat if you keep people in your closest circle that undervalue you in a way that might have you questioning your worth. When people treat us in a way that's disconnected from how we value ourselves, it's because we've trained them to do so by allowing them to violate our boundaries, compromise our standards, and disregard the respect we deserve. From that compromised state, it's impossible to maintain the courage necessary to move forward.

Too often we'll justify allowing the behavior because of time served, excusing their actions because of love. Love isn't a hall pass to treat you poorly. Knowing someone for a long time, even family, doesn't give permission to engage below your standards.

As author and motivational speaker Tony Gaskins said, "You teach people how to treat you by what you allow, what you stop, and what you reinforce." I'll say it another way: Sometimes you have to shoot a hostage. Sometimes you have to put someone on notice.

The only way the people in your life will know the kind of respect you expect, the kind of boundaries you need, and the kind of standards you hold for how you need to be treated is if you're consistently clear about two things: how you value yourself and your every-single-time unwillingness to let someone come into your space if they can't treat you the way you deserve. Those who can't need distance or departure.

Do you struggle to stand up for yourself when you've been mistreated? Do you feel guilty about prioritizing self-care? Do you spend your time trying to meet the needs of others who take more than you give? Can you relate to feeling like you're being taken for granted?

If you answered yes to any of these questions, you need to ask yourself why the people in your life feel they have license to treat you this way. And you must determine what steps are necessary to keep your values intact. Knowing your value and setting boundaries to protect it is an act of self-love. As author and speaker Brené Brown says, "Daring to set boundaries is about having the courage to love ourselves, even when we risk disappointing others." Your decision to draw a line in the sand and to maintain your boundaries is the only way to keep *you* intact.

LOGBOOK

JOURNALING ACTIVITY

Consider the following questions and record whatever comes to you in your journal.

- Who is trying to negotiate you into accepting a lower value for yourself than what you deserve?
- What kind of conversations do you need to have with these people in order to hold the line for your worth?

YOUR
IDENTITY

For more than two decades I held roles in the entertainment business. At a family gathering or a night out with friends, I was known by the stories I'd tell from the experiences I had working on a popular TV show, the craziness of managing actors and recording artists, and ultimately as the guy who worked at Disney. At the end of my run at the mouse house, as I left traditional media for an unconventional start-up, the identity I'd known for so long was gone in an instant. It was jarring. Leaving your safe harbor usually is.

GETTING TO KNOW MY SELF

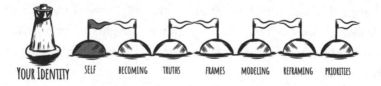

YOUR IDENTITY   SELF   BECOMING   TRUTHS   FRAMES   MODELING   REFRAMING   PRIORITIES

In a similar way, for sixteen years, a core part of my identity was being married, being a husband. Especially in the years after leaving Hollywood, whenever I met someone new, one of the first things I'd say in describing myself was, "I'm Rachel's husband." This meant that, after our divorce, I found myself again in the midst of an identity crisis, much like the stay-at-home parent whose kids leave for college or the career executive who's been downsized out of the company. Out of the safe harbor yet again.

Who am I now that I'm no longer who I was?

Divorce wasn't something I'd ever imagined for myself, and the flood of grief I experienced when our marriage ended was overwhelming. At the time of my divorce, I had been in therapy for years, but I found that I needed someone new to help me through this particular crisis. I needed someone to help me figure out who I was, now that I could no longer define myself by our marriage. I needed to find my *self.*

In my initial intake call with David, who would eventually become my new therapist and a crucial part of my life, he described his method. I'll admit, it sounded incredibly strange to me at first:

> How would it feel to disclose shameful feelings to others if you could say "Part of me feels . . ." rather than "I feel . . ."? What if you totally trusted that those parts were different from your true self and that you, as that self, could help them to transform? This is the approach of Internal Family Systems (IFS), a therapeutic method that helps you understand the various parts of yourself, how they work together, and how you can take control of those parts so they collaborate to drive your personal growth.

This may sound a bit odd, but he was asking me to imagine that my thoughts and feelings come from totally distinct, individual parts inside of me that *weren't me.* Setting aside how strange it sounded at first, I tried to connect to what good might be possible if I were to think of my psyche as having discrete parts. How might it change the way I thought about who I am if I were certain that my most vile thoughts about myself came from little pieces of me playing a role instead of being the core of my whole identity?

As much as I get this now, when David and I first spoke, I was a mess, spinning and crying. His explanation was lost on me. My response to him was, "Look, I don't know who I am, I don't understand what I'm feeling, and I hate what I'm thinking. Got anything for that?"

David stayed calm and talked me down, explaining that this IFS approach was a great match for the work I was looking to do. He said it in a way that has stuck with me ever since. "Imagine that you are the sun," he told me. "Floating all around you are your thoughts, your inner dialogue, your emotions and your experiences. In our analogy these things are the clouds. When we go through a dark period where we feel like we've lost ourselves, it's because these clouds presented themselves in a way that blocked out the light for so long that we forget the sun even existed. The clouds are doing their best to protect and take care of you, but given that they aren't even aware of the sun, they find it hard to give space. However, once they start to know the sun, they create a relationship that gives them permission to relax, trusting the self can take the lead."

I was intrigued. And desperate.

So we began our work together. It was the start of a journey that over this past year has led me to a place of peace and healing that would never have been possible otherwise. Through our sessions, I've come to understand that we all have a self, and we all have parts (our thoughts, emotions, and actions). This way of understanding myself and my feelings has made me feel normal at the most abnormal time of my life. Among the most reassuring ideas behind IFS are:

- The self has the opportunity to act as a mediator between these various parts.
- Every part of ourselves, even our negative thoughts or unhealthy behaviors, is something to welcome and make a relationship with to understand what important role each part believes it is playing to keep us safe.

Let me give you a specific example of how this plays out in my life with regard to anxiety. For the longest time, whenever anxiety would present itself in my life, I'd either suppress it, spin out from it, or take it out on the people I care about in my personal or professional life. But through the insights of this work, I am able to mediate my relationship with anxiety. I can take a step back and ask the anxiety why it is showing up and what role it believes it is there to play. When I become a mediator in the interaction between my self and this part of who I am, I can ask my anxiety, "What's up?"

My anxiety typically presents itself when there is a part of my life where I don't yet have a plan for how to work through a particular challenge. The role that anxiety is trying to play is that of intel officer, reporting that this ambiguity in this portion of my life exists, so that my self will address it and develop a better plan for achieving my goals.

Almost miraculously, this work has transformed the relationship I have with my thoughts and emotions from dread and frustration to gratitude for the insights they provide, even when they aren't necessarily positive or pleasant in and of themselves. By recognizing that my feelings are there to help me, but that they are not me, I am able to find courage in the midst of chaos. I am able to separate who I am from what I think or feel. IFS teaches that the self has ten powerful qualities (the 10 Cs) that enable us to take on the most challenging situations and the trickiest moving pieces of our parts. When isolated from our thoughts and feelings, the self is calm, confident, curious, clear, courageous, creative, consistent, connected, compassionate, and content. I mean, who doesn't want these characteristics on display every single day?

As an accomplice to this therapy work, the most important book I read in this past very hard year was *The Untethered Soul* by Michael Singer. It's not a new book, but the profound nature of this complementary message was liberating for me as I wrestled with what I felt and why I thought the way I did in the midst of struggle. The biggest takeaway: the idea that each of us should "untether" our feelings and that inner dialogue in our head from our true selves. As Singer says in the book, "There is nothing more important to true growth than realizing that you are not the voice of the mind—you are the one who hears it."

These ideas feel revolutionary as we jump into a conversation around identity. You are not your thoughts. You are not your emotions. You are an observer of them. If you are willing to build a relationship with them, if you are willing to listen to the data they present without reacting rashly to the signals they're sending, you will begin to see these parts as helpers that will give you the courage to sail into rough waters.

LOGBOOK

JOURNALING ACTIVITY

Take my anxiety example and apply it to yourself. Think back to the last time you experienced anxiety and try to separate your feelings from your self in that moment. Treat that anxiety as if it were a person you were sitting down to meet with. Give a name to your anxiety if you need to (mine is named Clark). Now ask your anxiety what information it's trying to offer you. What role does it believe it is playing? In your journal, record the answers that come to you and ask yourself whether there is a way to turn those negative feelings into a hopeful plan.

THE FOUR GATES OF BECOMING

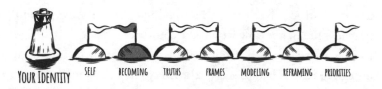

YOUR IDENTITY   SELF   BECOMING   TRUTHS   FRAMES   MODELING   REFRAMING   PRIORITIES

In reframing who I am and why I'm here in the midst of sea change, I also turned to some friends for their advice on how to come to grips with my new identity. My first call was to my friend, bestselling author and performance coach Brendon Burchard. He introduced me to his Four Gates of Becoming: Awareness, Acceptance, Accountability, and Action.

Gate of Awareness

Under the headline "Know Thyself" start by asking "who am I?" Not who you are to other people, but who you are at your core.

This was where I first understood that I had departed from who I truly was. I had lost touch with "me." In this gate, I had to become an observer of the patterns and loops, the habits and routines running my life. I took on the courage to confront the things I didn't currently like about myself, such as shame and regret, the disappointment of unkept promises I had made with myself. It's also here that I homed in on what it is that makes me proud, where my joy comes from, the times when I feel best about myself when I'm by myself.

For me, the Gate of Awareness presented itself in the work of staying connected to who I know I am at my core, as well as the hyper awareness of the ways my humanity can discredit these truths. This duality breeds the courage to move forward because of the clarity that awareness affords.

To step into who I'm meant to be, I needed to connect with my foundational truths and be radically honest about how I was getting in my own way. Knowing who I am and how I'm wired keeps me focused on where I'm heading and what it will uniquely take for me to get there. Understanding the ways I might undermine the pursuit gives me a fighting chance to preemptively keep any unwanted sabotage from happening before it does.

Gate of Acceptance

Next, comes an act of surrender. Not giving up, but letting go. Fully accepting how life is, not how we wish it could be.

It was hard for me to confront how little we control, giving permission for my ego to relax. I had to accept the things that happened and appreciate that all the good that will come in my future will have been built on top of everything I learned from both the positive and negative experiences of my past. The intended outcome of this gate is to give yourself permission to just be. I had to acknowledge that I am already whole. Already worthy, enough, valuable, and capable today, no matter where. No, not every circumstance in life delivers what I hope for, but things are as they are, and the challenge is to find the good in the now.

In the months after leaving Disney, there were moments when I felt lost. But in leaving my career for my calling, I also felt myself found. I was overwhelmed at the prospect of mapping out a new future in the aftermath of my marriage, but also exhilarated by the prospect of creating something new and connected to who I truly am. I couldn't change my circumstances. Neither lamenting my divorce (something I did not choose) nor stressing over leaving Disney (something I did choose) would support where I was heading. Acceptance is a choice to let go of what was so that you can get to the work of what will be.

Gate of Accountability

Once we know where we are and accept that we're there, we can take our power back. The power to control our thoughts and our actions. The certainty in our ability to handle what's next, cultivating the courage required to do what it will take to manufacture the vision we have for our future.

It's at the Gate of Accountability where you start to become the captain of your ship. It's here that you decide how you'll steer into the waves and weather the storms ahead with the mindset, habits, discipline, and community that it will take. Come face-to-face with the importance of having agency over your life.

For me, it was important that owning the role I would play in moving forward didn't have me veering toward regret because I hadn't started sooner. Feeling shame or loathing for the chaotic state I was moving away from did not serve where I was headed. It's called *becoming* for a reason. It happens in time, through experience and regularly learning from mistakes in the unknown.

Gate of Action

Ownership acts as a catalyst for change. Having cast a new vision for where you're headed and who you have to be to get there leaves a trail of breadcrumbs for making that vision a reality every day. This is the shift that asks, "Now that the game moving forward has changed, how has the playbook changed?"

Here you're intentionally controlling all vital energies to create alignment between who you want to be and how you show up each day. Delivering integrity in your actions today to become the person you hope to be tomorrow. We'll dive into this idea more as we hit the upcoming chapters on habits and routines.

• • •

The journey of becoming your true self is a process, an evolution that takes place over time and goes through the stages that require you to come to understand:

- Where you are.
- That you cannot change what has been.
- That you take accountability for what is required next.
- That you take the steps to actually make it happen.

In your pursuit to step into your version of becoming the full you, consider how awareness, acceptance, accountability, and action will help bolster the courage you'll need for the work that lies ahead.

LOGBOOK

JOURNALING ACTIVITY

Now I'll ask you the same questions Brendon asked me. Jot down your answers in your journal.

- How much self-awareness do you possess? How well do you know yourself?
- Can you surrender to the reality that the things that have happened to you in the past can't be changed?
- Are you willing to take accountability for what it will take to move ahead?
- Can you turn that decision into action in how you show up today?

TRUTHS WITH A CAPITAL T

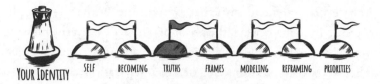

YOUR IDENTITY   SELF   BECOMING   TRUTHS   FRAMES   MODELING   REFRAMING   PRIORITIES

Perhaps it's fitting that on two of my past three Father's Days, I've found myself grappling with some big questions surrounding my identity. The irony isn't lost on me that the day that recognizes one of the most stable and proud parts of my life, being a dad to these four kids, might also hold space for two challenging inflection points in my evolution.

The End of an Era

On Father's Day in 2018, the trigger was the end of my seventeen-year career at Disney Studios. For the previous eight years, Father's Day weekend for me meant being involved in a big film industry event called CineEurope, which had me traveling to cities like Barcelona or Amsterdam to present the latest and greatest from Disney, Marvel Studios, Lucasfilm, and Pixar Animation. Pixar also traditionally released a blockbuster family movie on Father's Day weekend, which meant that as head of sales, who also doubled as press spokesman for the company, I was working around the clock rather than spending the holiday with my children.

I left Disney on May 30, 2018. Two weeks later, it was my successor waking up in Europe to pitch the company's next big projects while I sat on my living-room floor drinking coffee out of the mug that my kids had just given me on our first Father's Day together in nearly a decade. I was beyond grateful for the time with my kids, but I was also wrestling with the weight of my decision to leave the identity of that big job behind me.

Redefining Family

Two years later, on May 30, 2020, I woke up in a hotel room where Rachel and I had stayed the night before to celebrate our sixteenth wedding anniversary. After returning from a long walk, she mustered the courage to announce that our marriage had "run its course." The problem, she said, wasn't one big thing, but a thousand small ones. In the moment I could barely comprehend what that even meant. We had a triumph of a partnership in so many ways, the proof of which came in the blessings of our four kids and all of our memories and adventures together. I pleaded with her to try couples counseling or a trial separation; or that we could make it work if I fully extricated myself from the company we worked on together, taking my stepping away from day-to-day leadership to launch my book and coaching some six months earlier to a further level. But she had made her decision and I found myself facing the loss of another identity.

Three weeks later, Father's Day 2020 arrived. While some of the initial shock of Rachel's announcement had begun to wear off, my grief was ripe. I was struggling to adjust my sails for this new course that was taking hold. That Father's Day would be my first one alone with the kids. I felt as if I'd been thrown into the deep end of being a single dad. Two years after walking away from my professional identity, I was out in the choppy waters of a new sea that had chosen me. And it was just as disorienting.

In each case, I felt completely unmoored. The massive pillar of my identity was knocked down, and I no longer knew who I was. In 2018, I had chosen to push off from a harbor. In 2020, I was grasping to hold onto a dock that I didn't want to leave, even if time would show me that staying anchored wasn't good for either one of us.

I had to regain my equilibrium in both moments of identity crisis. I had to ask myself: *Who am I now that I'm not who I've been?* I had to figure out the pillars of my identity that were incapable of falling, that would stand strong irrespective of the conditions they were forced to endure. These pillars would become my Truths with a capital T.

Child of God

Father to four exceptional kids

Son, brother, friend

Co-parent with an extraordinary woman

Advocate

A guy doing his best every day to bring impact through his work

These were my Truths that I knew could withstand any storm. That would never falter, regardless of how my external circumstances changed.

As you contemplate your identity, and your capital-T Truths, I encourage you to remember that becoming your full, true self has been ordained by something greater than you. My identity starts with my faith in something greater than myself. In the recognition of that first and most important truth, everything else falls into place.

James 4:8 from the Bible reads, "Come near to God and he will come near to you." While I respect that you might not believe in the higher power that I do, I encourage you to connect first with something beyond yourself for strength. In the midst of challenges to your identity, the decision to lean into and intentionally create closeness to your creator will give you a feeling of actually being closer. The control we lose in identity change gives way to surrender. It's in that surrender that we are afforded a certainty only available from a higher power beyond ourselves.

Similar to the way that I hope you will tap into the strength of a higher power, I encourage you to seek out the support of the people in your life who believe that you were created for great purpose. This will give you the courage to believe it yourself and to unlock your already present, preordained potential.

My daughter Noah and I have a ritual called Tea Time where I try to take the concepts I teach adults and break them down in a way that she can comprehend. I use this time together to extol the limitless possibilities of her dreams, the power of believing in herself, and the fact that she has been prequalified for a life that unleashes her gifts. This is my attempt to support her in a way that will allow her to recognize her full potential as she grows.

Regardless of your belief system, I want you to recognize that your identity is much wider and deeper than a title on a business card or your relationship status. These are things that can be taken from us in a minute, and that will leave us lost at sea if we cling too tightly to them. We must find a way to connect with something bigger than ourselves, a sense of identity that can withstand any storm.

I don't know what my next Father's Day will have in store for me. But I do know that my ability to survive and thrive, come what may, is contingent on staying connected to my capital-T truths and my faith in a power greater than my own to guide me along the way.

LOGBOOK

JOURNALING ACTIVITY

Consider the list of capital–T Truths that I made for myself. Can you make a list of your own? Grab your journal and jot down a list of the Truths that will always stand strong for you, regardless of external factors in your life. Then ask yourself, "Is my list of Truths connecting me with something greater than myself?"

I AM NOT WHO YOU SAY I AM

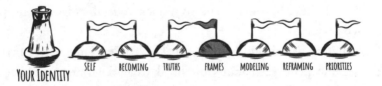

YOUR IDENTITY   SELF   BECOMING   TRUTHS   FRAMES   MODELING   REFRAMING   PRIORITIES

In this work surrounding identity that we're doing, we have to become detectives of sorts, sifting through our limiting beliefs in ourselves about who we are "supposed" to be, and figuring out where they've come from. Only then can we put them behind us. Often when we're feeling frustrated and unfulfilled, the source of our discontent can be traced back to the gap that exists between who we are at our core and how we feel like we have to show up to get affirmation from outside sources. It's exhausting.

In order to get to the bottom of it, let's start by digging down into the sources of who we think we're supposed to be. Call them rules, norms, systems, agreements, or anything else. From childhood, each of us is indoctrinated in a set of guiding principles that tell us how to be, sometimes at the expense of who we were meant to be. The challenge comes in doing the work to break free from stories that keep us in our own way or from programming that was imposed on us that contradicts our purpose. The goal is to replace those stories and programming with a new set of guiding principles that align with our values, passions, competencies, calling, and interest in unleashing our light into the world.

We are all influenced by the voices of authority in our lives, including parents, teachers, friends, and religious leaders. We are also shaped by broader societal forces that attempt to define what success looks like, what being a "good mom," a "real man," or a "productive member of society" means. But if we recognize that these forces do not have the final say, we can begin to release ourselves from these limiting roles and claim a new identity. An identity true to who we really are and were meant to be.

We don't get to choose the family we're born into, the religion we're brought up in, or the values held by those around us. But as adults, we must find the courage to question whether the rules that were put on us as children still serve us as adults, in our family, in this millennium. We have to determine whether the beliefs handed down to us align with our personal values, our future goals, and the vision of who we hope to become.

This can be tricky because there is an underlying reward/punishment cycle involved in these beliefs. When we conform to our assigned roles, we're often showered with praise. But when we step out of line, we may find ourselves subjected to harsh criticism and judgment. So we must ask what good is praise and approval if it keeps us from becoming our true selves and living in line with our calling? How fulfilled can you ever really be if praise comes with a condition to deny who you really are?

The only way to break free from this reward/punishment cycle is to establish a new set of beliefs, or *operating principles* as I called them in my last book, that serve who we're meant to be, and that are aligned with our values. Releasing yourself from what no longer serves you and establishing the principles that set you up for who you hope to become requires that you break it down in steps:

1. Take inventory of the beliefs that you have that are rooted in fear, that keep you docked in your safe harbor, or that make you question your worthiness of reaching for the life you deserve. As much as these may have existed from the time we were children, freedom will come in pulling them apart and leaving them behind.

2. Find a way to release yourself from the power that your old limiting beliefs may hold over you by both challenging the credibility of the source and the relevance of the rule in your life today. Does the source of this belief have credibility generally? If so, does it have credibility on your specific set of circumstances? Does the belief, which may have been born and made sense in the 1970s while you were growing up in your parents' house in an era governed by different cultural norms, still have relevance in the world that you live in today? Is it relevant to your personal values?

3. Make peace with what was. You will not reap the benefits of this freedom if you keep yourself anchored with shame for having believed what you did, or anger toward those who imposed these limitations on you. Give yourself grace, and with a spirit of forgiveness for the people and structures that held you back, move forward in freedom.

Learning to Run

An example of a time when I had to reframe one of my limiting beliefs, and which I discuss in my last book, was challenging a notion I'd held for more than thirty-five years that I wasn't cut out to be a runner. This was something that I had believed since childhood, and it wasn't until I questioned where this belief came from that I was able to reframe that limitation and turn it into something empowering.

In this instance, the belief came from my mother. She is the most incredible woman and is so full of love for me that this belief was presented as love, though told through the lens of her fear. She had watched some-one else she loved and who was tall injure themselves while running, and she was concerned that since I, too, was tall, I might injure my back or my knees or hips. She took the truth of someone else's experience, bolstered by her fear for my safety, wrapped it in love, and handed it to me.

As much as I love my mother and know that she had the best of inten-tions, when I decided to challenge this belief, after determining where it had come from, I then had to question the credibility of my source. My mother is not a runner, she is not tall, and she is not running in my body. So she did not have the credibility to decide on my truth in this situation. This gave me full permission to test the hypothesis of my own truth: that I might, indeed, be cut out for running after all.

So at age thirty-six I began running. Short distances at a slow pace to start, but I ran. And when I did not experience the feared pain in my back or my knees or my hips, I ran more. Longer distances. At a faster pace. I have become a runner who in this past year ran more than twenty half marathons and a full marathon, my first. Running has become a mix of exercise, therapy, and church for me, for its physical, mental, and spiritual benefits. I would never have discovered my truth—I am a runner—had I not challenged this limiting belief and the credibility of its storyteller (I love you, Mom). And this truth has unlocked so much for me, leading me to get to the bottom of other "truths" in my life that required rewriting.

We are all a product of our programming. Any time we run into outdated code, it's our job to write an update and download it as often as we can until the alternative is fully obsolete.

The Placebo Effect of Misdiagnosis

I tend to be a fan of personality indicator tests like the Love Language quiz, and the Enneagram and DiSC tests as tools for better understanding our strengths versus the areas where we need to grow. With that said, I have also experienced the pitfalls of using one of these tests to self-diagnose. When I was writing my last book, I decided to take an Enneagram test to better understand myself, and it got me into some trouble.

When I took the test, I was identified as a "nine," a *peacekeeper,* some-one who is known to be accepting and trusting, willing to go along with whatever others need to keep the peace. After accepting the results of this diagnostic, I found myself behaving in a way that was unusually conflict-avoidant for me, constantly trying to make things go smoothly. I later discovered that when you take this test in a season of stress, a person who traditionally identifies as a "three," an *achiever*, can score as a nine. I had taken this test during a stressful time of my life and in doing so I got a result that wasn't true to who I am. I am a three who tested as a nine.

The cautionary tale: I had accepted the diagnosis of this "expert" test, and the power of suggestion led me to bend my personality to fit results that were not really true for me. I read the qualities of what it means to be a peacekeeper and, on some level, both conscious and unconscious, I began adapting my behavior to match what I'd been told.

This reminds me of the way we approach many things in life. Our parents define what it means to be a good son or daughter. Our school defines what makes a great student. Our church defines what it means to be a good parishioner. Our society tells us what it means to be a good citizen. And the wild thing is, when we hear what these voices of authority have to say, on some level we find ourselves conforming in order to be accepted, even when it comes at the expense of our true selves.

The lesson here is that we must always question the values that are handed down to us, whether in the form of a parent's well-intentioned warning, or the results of a less-than-scientific personality test. At the end of the day, the goal isn't to conform to someone else's identity or society's prescription for what to believe. Instead we must always question external forces, push back on the constructs that don't honor who we were created to be, and forge an identity and a set of beliefs all our own.

LOGBOOK

JOURNALING ACTIVITY

Consider whether you may have accepted fear-based, limiting beliefs about yourself that are keeping you from living your truth. Take the "tall people can't be runners" example. Is there a version of this for you? It's time to trace back the origins of that belief and test your hypothesis. Ask yourself:

- Where did these beliefs originate for me? Who was the storyteller?
- Was the storyteller a trusted person in my life who may have had good intentions? Did they have credibility?
- In what ways are these beliefs keeping me from living my truth?
- Can I find the courage to test the validity of these beliefs and to break free from them?

WHAT WILL THIS DO TO YOUR KIDS?

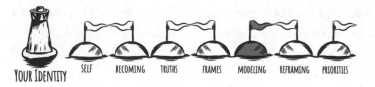

YOUR IDENTITY   SELF   BECOMING   TRUTHS   FRAMES   MODELING   REFRAMING   PRIORITIES

As you think about the things that may get in the way of your ambition to step fully into who you were meant to be, there will be plenty of times when you'll worry about the impact that heeding this call may have on the people you love most. How might your husband or wife react to you deciding to pursue something for you if the version of who you become deviates from the person that you've historically been? How might your friends react if your decision to commit to the steps necessary for unlocking your passion comes at the expense of being readily available for nightly Netflix co-binges or meetups at a bar or one of a hundred things that were nice but not necessarily using your time and energy in a way that aligned with your values to propel you forward?

There will be pangs of guilt and pressures to conform to how you're *supposed* to be for those you're supposed to love in a certain way that was likely determined by the programming downloaded to you throughout your life. As much as we just talked about questioning the sources of that programming and challenging the credibility of the stories, structures, and frames it created in your life, it's something that is going to be particularly triggering when you think about how your decisions impact your kids. As much as we'll talk in an upcoming chapter about releasing yourself from the worry of what other people think, some of their judgment is easier to let go of than others. The worry of judgment around how we parent is among the hardest to shake.

I'd love to tell you that this issue is as much a challenge for moms as it is for dads, but you know that's not the case. Mommy guilt is a corrosive, toxic poison that will undoubtedly have the women who read this book affected in a way that men have not experienced, and may not even be totally conscious of. Daddy guilt, on the other hand, is, well, nonexistent. Or, if it does exist, it's nothing compared to the standards, expectations, and feelings that women inevitably endure.

When Rachel and I were building a company to place tools in hands to help people have a better life, she got a question that I never got. The fact that she was asked over and over while I never got the question makes it worthy of a conversation here today. The question was: "What will this do to your children?"

As in, as a woman who was listening to her intuition, following her passion, unlocking her potential in a way that might honor her creator, what would the long hours do to the kids? Though it was this very creator who intentionally filled her with these gifts, this drive, and her ambition, what would all this work, the travel, the decision to lean into the opportunity to bring her light to the world do to our children?

I built a career in entertainment for twenty-five years, working hard, putting in long hours, at one point leading the international sales force that required many a visit to our seventy-five offices around the world. In the aftermath, I jumped into scaling The Hollis Company and found myself again following my passion, putting in the hard work and long hours, and flying from city to city. Yet I never once got asked the question.

It was the by-product of the patriarchal society that we've been raised in, the cultural expectations that are applied to one gender and not another. But in wrestling with this phenomenon, there are three big observations that I want to draw the attention of the women reading this in the hope that you don't let this double standard stop you from unlocking your gifts. Men, understanding and appreciating these three points is important for you if you're hoping to support the women you love and be accomplices in changing the broader programming in society so that the light that will come from these women can reach their intended recipients.

1. You were born this way. The intuition, passion, drive, ambition, and everything else was placed there by design. It was not a mistake that it existed; it was intention. The whisper from the voice in your gut is trying to encourage you to honor the intention of your design. To create integrity between how you were made, the purpose for your life, and how you actually live. The world may try to talk you out of honoring the measure of your intended creation, but every day you live with the dissonance of those external voices rather than your internal one, you do so in a posture that discounts the creator and sacrifices your chances for fulfillment.

2. Any question that only applies to women but not men, or to men but not women, is not a question worthy of answering. That I never had the same question asked, never had to experience the discomfort of feeling guilty about pursuing my passion or unlocking my potential, makes the question to Rachel a false premise. That its foundation was built on a double standard means giving weight to the answer in any meaningful way affords it credibility that it does not deserve.

3. The entire question changes when you alter the tone of how it is being asked. When I would tell this story onstage at our conferences, I would yell as loud I could, *"What will this do to our kids!?"* As the dad of three

boys, their mom following her heart and pursuing her dreams has told each of them that a woman is as entitled as a man to lead a boardroom, write *New York Times* bestselling books, stand on a stage in front of ten thousand people, and a hundred other things. As a dad to a young daughter, her mama's belief in herself and willingness to fully unlock the intended design of her creation gives permission for Noah to do the same. My kids will never think twice about what a woman can do because of the woman modeling all that's possible when you follow your heart.

In these last few months, as I've trained for the Iron Man, my kids have witnessed what it takes to get into the shape needed to not die on the course. When I get my running shoes on, it's not strange to have my eight-year-old Ford put his shoes on to see if he can make it on the first two miles of the loop. When I get out into the garage gym in the morning, I'm rarely working out alone because of what has become a usual routine of being followed by a small human who wants to work on his fitness too.

These kids are watching us. Watching what we do and absorbing it as programming for how they should be in the world. They will either take the model of you believing in yourself as the permission they need to believe in themselves, or will see the way you deny part of who you are to serve mommy guilt or play small for the worry of what "good girls do," and believe that's the way you're supposed to do it.

And, men, you can't have it both ways. You can't tell your daughter that she can be anything she believes she can be and then passive-aggressively punish your wife (whose ambition to bring light into this world makes you a little uncomfortable) for heeding her call. Your daughter sees both. The women in your life are light bearers. You can be an accomplice in the impact they'll make by supporting the full exploitation of their gifts and dreams. Many pieces of the double standard were created by and fueled by men over time, so if the double standard is going to go away, we're going to have to do our part to disassemble it.

At the end of the day, woman or man, we're teaching these kids to listen to their intuition, follow their passion, and fully step into who they were meant to be. Or we aren't. What will this do to your kids? Everything.

ACTIVITY

Make a list of the attributes you want to download to your kids. What kind of programming are you hoping they'll pick up now and carry into who they become? Once you have your list, have the courage to be honest about where there's alignment in your actions and the aspiration of your modeling. If the code you'd hope for them to believe in is disconnected from the code your operating system is running, you'll need to take a hard look in the mirror and commit to the firmware upgrade that brings the out-of-date code you're running up to speed.

LIABILITIES TO SUPERPOWERS

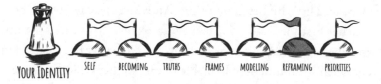

YOUR IDENTITY   SELF   BECOMING   TRUTHS   FRAMES   MODELING   REFRAMING   PRIORITIES

I have such a strange career. After two and a half decades of work in corporate offices that required me to wear a belt that matched my shoes, I'm now someone who rotates through four different colors of V-neck T-shirts as I segue from writing to coaching to recording podcasts. It's as hard to explain it to my grandmother as you'd expect. That said, the podcasting piece has been a surprisingly rewarding part of my work because of the perspective it has afforded me and the listeners of the show.

My podcast is called *Rise Together*. The idea behind it is to bring people into the recording studio who've had vastly different life experiences to share their journeys. The hope is to create an empathy bridge between their worldviews and those of the listener, so that we all move a step closer to putting ourselves in someone else's shoes.

Over the past year the show has featured the story of a widower persevering through grief after losing his wife to cancer; a hard conversation about mental health with a pastor's wife whose husband died by suicide; an episode featuring the parents of children with Down syndrome about celebrating people of all abilities; a mother's brave fight to destigmatize teen addiction; a man's stoic confrontation of a terminal Parkinson's disease diagnosis; a blind man's triumph through Harvard Business School; and so much more.

In every instance, these people who might otherwise have allowed their circumstances to define their identities in a negative way instead chose to use the unique lens through which they see the world as an opportunity for impact rather than a liability. As much as any single story could have been the focus of this chapter, there was one interview in particular that's forever left an imprint on me.

Just after I was first married, back when Rachel and I lived in Los Angeles, we went to a church where a couple named Katherine and Jay Wolf were leading a class called "Young Marrieds." They were a cool duo, doing their best to help kids like us who didn't know what they were doing in marriage get a little bit better over time. And then one day, just after giving birth to her first son, Katherine had a catastrophic stroke that she miraculously survived. Everything she had envisioned for her life changed in an instant when she found herself unable to care for her children as she had, confined to a wheelchair, and having to relearn how to do just about everything in her life. Since recovering from her stroke, she has spent over a decade serving communities who have experienced similar trauma, acting as a steady voice of hope and helping others to heal.

I invited Katherine and Jay to be guests on the podcast. In our conversation I was trying to understand how with the hand they'd been dealt they could stay so connected to hope. How had they been able to turn this thing that happened *to* them into something that happened *for* them? While it wasn't easy, the answer was simple. They told me that regardless of the circumstances presented, they turned to a Bible verse, and one I hadn't heard before, Habakkuk 3:17–18:

Though the fig tree does not bud and there are no grapes on the vines,
though the olive crop fails and the fields produce no food,
though there are no sheep in the pen and no cattle in the stalls,
yet I will rejoice in the Lord, I will be joyful in God my Savior.

Against convention, Katherine rewrote this scripture to fit her life as she lay in a hospital bed, recovering from her near-death experience, a new mother in a body that didn't work as it did before. Her version read:

Though I cannot walk and am confined to a wheelchair, though my face is paralyzed and I cannot smile, though I am extremely impaired and cannot take care of my own baby boy, yet I will rejoice in the Lord, I will be joyful in God my savior.

The conversation brought me to tears as I was myself in the midst of a sea change following the end of my marriage. So I did what she did: wrote my own version of this Bible verse (and I encourage you to do the same if this exercise resonates with you). Here is my version:

Though my marriage has come to an end and my future looks different than I thought it would, though this blank piece of paper I've been handed to imagine what's next fills me with equal parts fear and excitement, though my identity both at home and at work is shifting under my feet, yet I will rejoice in the Lord, I will be joyful in God my savior.

What I find interesting is that every one of the guests on my podcast could have written their own testimony to how they've decided to turn tragedy into triumph, pain into power, loss into a platform to help others feel less alone. When unexpectedly hard things happen in our lives, and they will, it's an intentional, conscious decision not to let that shift in our identity act as a sentence that constrains what's possible for our lives. It doesn't mean it will be easy or will in any way feel fair, but if we can fight to see adversity as something that's happening *for* us, as something that may allow us to help others as we shine a light through our pain, it just might turn the perceived liability into a superpower.

So let's turn the tables and ask ourselves how we can break through our limiting beliefs and transform our challenges into strengths. I'll give you an example from my own life.

Trial by Fire

When I was promoted to the head of sales for Disney Studios at age thirty-six, I didn't have the résumé to support the decision to put me in the role. Every person on my team had more experience than I did. The customers with whom I negotiated had been in the business for most of my life, and the filmmakers I was working with were accustomed to my predecessor, who with his thirty-plus years of experience had seen it all. There were plenty of stories that I could have believed from the voices in my head questioning whether I was up for the task.

The only way I could push past impostor syndrome was to reframe the story of why I could not only do the job, but why the experiences that I brought to the table made me uniquely qualified. It required taking my limiting beliefs and turning them into empowering beliefs. I had to reframe my stories to generate the courage necessary to do the job well.

It was true I didn't have the experience of most of my team, but I chose to believe that my fresh perspective as a curious newcomer would have us considering options that might not have occurred to us otherwise. In a relationship business, I was often introducing myself to my counterparts for the first time rather than catching up with them after a round of golf. But was it possible that being a relatively inexperienced, relatively unknown quantity could make me a more objective negotiator, better able to strike deals for the studio when things got tough? There was no doubt that my predecessor could walk into a room and reassure the filmmakers that his recommendation was the best, based on experience alone. I wondered whether my lack of experience could lead me to introduce a data and analytics team that would use math as a great equalizer in decision making. It did. And it worked.

I consciously chose to focus on my strengths in the way I reframed every story.

My questions to you are:

- What limiting stories are you telling yourself that may be keeping you from reaching your potential?
- How could you reframe these stories to focus on the strengths that make you uniquely qualified to chase your dreams?

Every limitation creates opportunity. Have the courage to turn your limitations into empowering stories of why you of all people are the one to chase the dreams in your heart. Your experiences have brought you here and made you who you are today. Honor them.

LOGBOOK

JOURNALING ACTIVITY

It is time to transform three of your limiting beliefs into stories of empowerment. I'll get you started with an example of how I did this back when I was promoted to head of sales at Disney. Then it's your turn.

MY LIMITING BELIEF: At age thirty-six, I lacked the years of experience and the long-standing industry relationships of my older colleagues.

MY EMPOWERING REFRAME: As a newcomer, I brought a fresh perspective to projects and built an analytics team; my lack of long-standing relationships with associates made me a more objective negotiator supported by data over emotion.

LOGBOOK

JOURNALING ACTIVITY
YOUR TURN

YOUR LIMITING BELIEF: _____
_____
_____

YOUR EMPOWERING REFRAME: _____
_____
_____

YOUR LIMITING BELIEF: _____
_____
_____

YOUR EMPOWERING REFRAME: _____
_____
_____

YOUR LIMITING BELIEF: _____
_____
_____

YOUR EMPOWERING REFRAME: _____
_____
_____

FIELD OF DREAMS

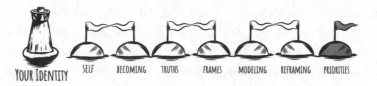

YOUR IDENTITY   SELF   BECOMING   TRUTHS   FRAMES   MODELING   REFRAMING   PRIORITIES

Author Nora Roberts was once asked about how she balanced work with having kids. She said, "The key to juggling is to know that some of the balls you have in the air are made of plastic and some are made of glass." The implication: some balls will drop. It's impossible to keep them all in the air all of the time because life is hard. Because standards are high. Because unexpected seasons introduce unexpected pain. When the inevitable happens, the key is to make sure you let the right balls hit the ground.

Two months into my divorce, I got an email from the commissioner of my son Sawyer's baseball league. The subject line had me shaking my head the second it hit my inbox: "Coaches Needed." In spite of all that I was juggling at the moment, I responded immediately: I was in. I sent it before I could think it through. Before I could be reasonable or practical or sane.

The old Dave would have declined. There was too much going on. Too many professional responsibilities and travel. Priorities for the "serious" stuff I'd deemed critical. These things were the glass balls that I wouldn't dare break. Or at least that's what I told myself, and in doing so I'd relegated coaching baseball to the plastic ball category.

Here's a little secret about the balls we juggle: We get to decide which are plastic and which are glass. We get to decide if the priorities of our lives align with our values or those of society. We get to decide what's "serious" to us.

So I officially became a little-league baseball coach. At a time when I had no clue what my life would look like from one week to the next, I made a snap decision to prioritize something that would help me connect to who I wanted to become: an even more involved father. And I didn't regret that decision for a minute. It was incredible to spend that time with my son and to be able to do something with him that my dad had done for me growing up.

It was my first time coaching little league and I had to figure things out on the fly. I learned about the scorebook you need as I got to the first game without one, scheduled a first practice on Labor Day (sorry, parents) and a second practice on the opening day of the NFL season (sorry, football fans). I used a YouTube video for infield practice inspiration and got to the last game still trying to figure out how to encourage small people without ending every sentence with "brother." It was a thing.

We lost our first four games of the season and got bounced from the playoffs before the trophy ceremony, but it was the absolute best. Every boy on that team improved, gave their all, and overcame setbacks in ways that will extend far beyond the ball field. Yes, those weeks where we found ourselves on the field four days in a row between practices and games felt a little intense, and yes, it was a lot to juggle with my other kids and work. But what happened on Field 4 of the local baseball fields was a miracle when I needed it most.

At a time in my life when I was struggling with my identity now that I was no longer a husband, feeling unmoored and trying to regain my sea legs, coaching little league was my anchor. Coaching those kids became a catalyst for jump-starting my courage and putting the pieces of my life back together. I know that if circumstances had been different, if I hadn't been in turmoil, I wouldn't have said yes to coaching. But with my identity in flux, I was willing to try it at a time when I needed to find new ways to create meaningful experiences with my kids. Thus, beauty was born from struggle: Coach Dave leading the Dripping Springs Rangers. Fortifying a pillar of my identity as dad to these kids that in this season would inevitably lead to a dirt track for go-karts out back, working our way through the series *Lost* (don't tell them about the finale), and so much more.

Crushing It

In the midst of this first season of coaching, another unexpected opportunity came my way. When we'd first moved from LA to Austin, just as I was leaving my career at Disney, I was asked to be an expert witness in a court case. I was just as surprised by the call as you may be reading these words.

It turned out that a lawsuit involving a movie theater had been filed and the defendants wanted someone with experience like mine to speak as an authority for the industry.

What followed was two years of intermittent work building my perspective on the facts of the case. Working through depositions and reading the testimony of other witnesses. Reams of information and hours of effort led to a twice postponed trial date. After weeks of prep, I was ready to take the stand, prepared to do my best to represent the depth of knowledge I had for an industry I'd been immersed in for the better part of my adult life.

And I've got to say, I crushed it on the stand. Taking questions from opposing counsel, I was at my best, giving answers and articulating my points in a way that illustrated my position and brought the most confident version of myself to life. It's not lost on me that two years of delays in the trial allowed this moment to arrive at a time when I desperately needed a confidence boost. It was great to be reminded of how strong I can be in my element, and how strong I would be in whatever came next. It also validated my departure from Disney. Even in the midst of this latest round of chaos, I knew I'd made the right decision. Taking the stand in my suit and tie threw me back into the midst of the movie business. It was a beautiful short-term return, but still a thing disconnected from my calling in life.

It also helped remind me that my qualifications for being an expert witness were built over decades. My ability to deliver on the stand would not have been possible without the effort, failure, discomfort, growth, and time that went into building my expertise. And the reminder that my expertise had developed over time and through struggle was a promise that it could all be built again.

I took the stand just after exiting The Hollis Company, trying to figure out what my next move would be. This experience gave me the courage and the confidence to walk toward effort and discomfort, to cast off into disorienting seas. Even in our most difficult times, when our identity has been tested and we're struggling to redefine who we are, I want to challenge you to do two things:

- Reconnect with something in your life that you can *crush*. This could be work-related or it could be an activity like bowling or gardening or singing in a choir. Find an area where you excel, where you have expertise; and when life pushes back or things fall apart, use this as a way to build confidence and remember who you are.

- Go Marie Kondo on your life and double down on the things that bring you joy while eliminating those that don't. Invest in the relationships that give your life meaning and the passions that light you up in order to cultivate the bravery needed to face your fears.

No matter what you're going through, joy is possible. Gratitude is something you can find if you look for it. Courage is something you can manufacture by connecting to your strengths and reminding yourself of how strong you have been in the past. And peace is available to you even in the midst of chaos when you stay focused on the priorities that matter most.

LOGBOOK

JOURNALING ACTIVITY

Create two lists. First name all of your "glass balls." What are the things you're juggling that cannot be dropped? Are the right things on the list? Second, name all the things you crush. How are you spending time connecting to your strengths to build the courage needed to be strong in the uncomfortable, disorienting parts of your life?

YOUR
EXPERIENCES

When I worked as the head of distribution at Disney, one of the surreal and delicate responsibilities of the job was taking the filmmakers and talent through the rationale behind where the film they'd just spent years of their life working on would land on a calendar. Surreal in the sense that I was dealing with some of the biggest names in the industry, people from Disney, Pixar, Lucas, and Marvel films whom I'd idolized since I was a kid. And delicate in that when you're a studio releasing blockbusters from such prolific brands, the quantity of big films in a year often outnumbered the number of "big film slots" on a calendar.

THE ROCK IN OCTOBER

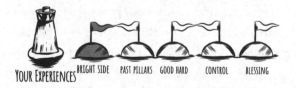

In early 2018 when it came time to schedule *The Jungle Cruise*, starring Dwayne "The Rock" Johnson, none of those magical big box-office spots were available. I knew there was nothing I could do to change that fact, and that I would have to deliver that news myself to The Rock. Yes, I would have to walk into a conference room and tell a man who had thrown men at least twice my size around a wrestling ring that his film was not going to be released in the summer. In addition to this Herculean task, I had to sell him on October, a month that was unproven when it came to box office success. For your reference, at the time of our meeting, the previous October had been the lowest moviegoing month of the calendar year.

A lot of prep would go into this meeting, and everyone involved knew one thing going in: The Rock loves to win. In every arena, he wants to be the very best. If I was going to have a chance at success, I'd have to put myself in his shoes and consider his perspective and motivations. I would have to convince him that with the marketing machine that is The Walt Disney Company, combined with beloved intellectual property and his unparalleled star power, we could create an event unlike anything the business had ever seen, regardless of when the film was released.

I went into this meeting armed with a solid plan for making my case, and with the facts. There was precedent at Disney for making a plan like this one a success. We'd opened Tim Burton's *Alice in Wonderland* in a previously unproven March back in 2010, Jon Favreau's *Jungle Book* in an unproven April in 2016, and had just shattered records with megahit *Black Panther* in an unproven February just months before this meeting. But still, I had to convince a megastar who was used to the red carpet treatment that this would work out.

The morning of our meeting, I strode into the conference room and began by greeting The Rock as "Dwayne." My first mistake. He said, "Call me DJ," which is apparently what people who are close to The Rock call him. Are you suggesting we might be *close* now? Regardless, I went on to present the competitive landscape for our proposed release date (there was no competition) and the focus for the company (we had no other big releases in September or October). I'd teed things up for the next question that I'd hoped DJ would ask. And ask he did: "What is the biggest movie of all time released in October?" At the time, the biggest October release of all time was George Clooney and Sandra Bullock's *Gravity*. It had made $56 million in its opening weekend in the United States and finished its run at a respectable $274 million. I knew that we'd need to do better to have this date make sense. Which led to DJ's second question: "If we release in October, could we be the biggest opening and biggest film of all time in the month?"

"Yes," I told him. "Yes, we could." He was fired up and on board. I was fired up and ready to make it work. As we ended the conversation, I thanked him. And I accidentally called him Dwayne. Again. He insisted that it was DJ. We're still not close. (And production delays and the pandemic eventually pushed the movie's release to July 2021.)

You may be wondering: How does this story about my very close personal friend DJ relate to the lessons in this book? This part of the book is called "Experiences," and in this section we'll discuss how we take any of our experiences in life and find the way to turn them, reframe them, into opportunities. You see, the circumstances of life are wildly beyond our control. You might sleep better at night by telling yourself that you have some power over what happens next, but in truth, you have none.

What you do have control over is how you turn the circumstances of your life into opportunities. Maximizing the good but also making lemonade out of lemons. As much as I would have preferred to confidently walk into that conference room and tell DJ about our plans for a Fourth of July or Thanksgiving release, the best I had to offer was October. But I believed in our plan. In the end, DJ got on board with my vision and took it a step further when he asked how he could turn it into the biggest and best of all time.

Similarly, I didn't ask for the 2020 that was handed to me. None of us did. But I'll be damned if I didn't turn it into the best year of my life. The posttraumatic growth that I stayed focused on was a catalyst for courage and a springboard for pursuing my next steps.

As we dive into the "Experiences" section of this book, can you begin to view the events in your life that you didn't necessarily plan for, that maybe you would never have hoped for, as having happened *for you* instead of *to you*? Can you choose to believe that the hand you've been dealt was meant to prepare you for where you're going rather than keep you stuck where you've been?

Life is hard. Experiences can often be unfair. But fairness is a construct that the universe doesn't understand and certainly doesn't play by. The way you give weight to your experiences can at times feel surreal. And delicate. When things don't go your way, will you see that as a sign to stop, or a sign to grow? In the end, the choice is yours. Choose wisely.

LOGBOOK

JOURNALING ACTIVITY

Think of something unexpected that happened in your life over the past year that produced pain, loss, or discomfort. Now try to list five positive things that eventually grew out of that experience. Can you expand that list into ten positive things and reframe the way you might even attach gratitude to the event?

CENTRAL VS. CIRCUMSTANTIAL EXPERIENCES

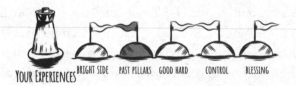

YOUR EXPERIENCES · BRIGHT SIDE · PAST PILLARS · GOOD HARD · CONTROL · BLESSING

In the Pixar movie *Inside Out*, the protagonist is an eleven-year-old girl named Riley. Through the magic of animation we get to see what's going on inside her mind. We see the "lands" that inform her identity, a visual representation of the experiences that have formed the way she sees herself and her life so far.

I like to imagine that all of us have these "lands" in our own minds, which represent the importance we attach to the experiences of our past. I like to refer to these core, foundational moments in our lives, whether positive or negative, as our "central experiences." These central experiences shape the way we value ourselves and the possibilities in our lives. These experiences in many ways define who we are. Or who we think we are.

In my last book, I quoted the motivational speaker Les Brown who once said, "Hope in the future is power in the present." I love this quote and may very well use it in my next book too.

Those wise words are telling us that if you can maintain an optimistic vision of what is possible for your life, the power of that hope will help you to live more fully today. But if there's hopelessness in the way that you've assigned value to the experiences of your past, or if there's hopelessness in the way that you currently think about your station in life, your vision for the future will be compromised. An incredibly tough place from which to build courage or create momentum.

You have to do the hard work of making peace with the experiences of your past. Did these things happen *to* you or *for* you? Have you climbed atop these failures or do you find yourself submerged beneath them? Is it possible to reframe the things you've been through as the requisite learning required for your future?

Achieving your goals for the future starts with believing in yourself. Your past experiences act as identity anchors, informing your beliefs about what you can achieve. As I see it, these past experiences come in two varieties: central experiences and circumstantial experiences.

Central Experiences

Our central experiences are like the lands in Riley's head. These are the fundamental and foundational experiences that define who we are and what we believe we're capable of. For example, you might not have gotten good grades in school. If that experience ends up being something that you've afforded positive attribution, perhaps by saying, "I got my degree in street smarts and have always figured things out," then you can parlay that perspective into courage. And that courage can fuel you to figure out anything that comes next. But if you attribute negativity to that experience by telling yourself, "Since I didn't get good grades I probably won't get this job or go far in this career," that becomes a fear-fueled self-fulfilling prophecy.

Our central experiences can be connected to how much money we had or didn't have growing up, how involved or absent our parents were, how we have been treated in relationships, and so on. Reframing the negative experiences of our past isn't intended to diminish the pain and trauma that they may have caused. The idea is to honor these experiences, viewing them as sources of strength and resilience, and ourselves as warriors who are braver for having survived them.

Circumstantial Experiences

Circumstantial experiences, on the other hand, are things that *happened to have happened*. Yes, they are part of our past, and yes, we may have some learnings that came from the processing of these experiences, but they do not define who we are. They are the color commentary to the story of our life, not the definition of what our life has meant.

In the example of getting good grades or not, someone whose identity isn't defined in any way by their grade point average has effectively attributed that experience as circumstantial. It happened to have happened.

It's important to make the distinction because our central experiences are often the source of our beliefs. Those beliefs can be limiting and hold us back; or empowering and propel us forward. Our ability to acknowledge how we've given weight to what we've been through and see the way that weight has acted as a catalyst or constraint can make the difference between moving forward or staying stuck.

For now the challenge for us all is to spend time grappling with how we've attributed positive or negative meaning to the central experiences of our past. And we have two main options for thinking about anything that currently limits how we believe in our worthiness and our ability to chase down our dreams:

- *We can choose to reframe the negative attribution we've given to a past experience in order to view this experience as something that gives us strength.* This doesn't mean some rose-colored glasses version of toxic positivity. This is us as the author of the stories that we tell ourselves writing something new. Something that empowers us to believe that even the things that happen for reasons we don't understand can be leveraged for purpose. An I've-been-forged-in-the-fire, I'm-a-freaking-warrior-now kind of purpose. An I'll-share-my-pain-to-give-others-hope kind of purpose. An I-didn't-deserve-it-but-I'm-gonna-use-it-for-fuel kind of purpose. This is the kind of learning that comes through perseverance, the kind of strength that's built in tenacity, the kind of skills we're afforded in survival. Courage is cultivated in it all, and you are the author of the story. You choose what story you write.

- *We can actively try to move a central experience into the circumstantial experience category.* To things that happened to have happened. The weight that we give to the experiences that define us only exists if we allow it. That won't diminish the pain or anguish; it won't discount the unfairness or trauma. But we can remove the power from something we went through if we make a hard decision not to allow it to have control over the balance of our lives. It's not easy, but with time, effort, therapy, community, and faith, it is possible.

There are many things in my life that fundamentally dictated how I believed myself to be good enough or not, worthy of the pursuit for more or unequipped. I had to assign meaning to my past experiences. When I allowed those experiences to act as evidence of what wasn't possible, I found proof of that insufficiency. But the opposite was also true: when I freed myself of the negative meaning I'd previously allowed weight for, the proof of that previous belief was something that no longer presented itself in my everyday life. Courage ensued. The same can be true for you.

How do we attempt to make that shift from central to circumstantial? It can come through:

- Taking power back by owning what we've been through with pride versus shame.
- Radical acceptance that affords something in peaceful liberation.
- Choosing to forgive someone who wronged you, and/or forgiving yourself.
- Finding community with others whose empathy normalizes our journey.

- Breakthroughs that come in therapy and journaling.
- The act of surrender to a higher power.

At the end of the day, the question you need to ask is: What are the stories you're telling about your past? Are these stories that limit what's possible or allow what's next? As the author, you have the opportunity to write anything you decide. The way you tell the story of what you've been through will make the difference in how you write the chapters that lie ahead.

LOGBOOK

JOURNALING ACTIVITY

Spend time thinking about the story of your life so far and examining the central experiences of your past. What have you been through that defines how you think of yourself? For each of these formative experiences, jot down the answers to the following questions:

- Is the story I'm telling myself a vehicle for empowerment? Or is this story an anchor that is holding me back?
- For a central experience that has negative associations, is there a way to reframe what you learned? Did your struggle allow you to gain strength or warrior status? Could it move to circumstantial?

CENTRAL EXPERIENCE & POSITIVES/NEGATIVES

_____
_____
_____
_____
_____

REFRAME OR MOVE TO CIRCUMSTANTIAL

_____
_____
_____

CENTRAL EXPERIENCE & POSITIVES/NEGATIVES

_____
_____
_____
_____
_____

REFRAME OR MOVE TO CIRCUMSTANTIAL

_____
_____
_____

CENTRAL EXPERIENCE & POSITIVES/NEGATIVES

_____
_____
_____
_____
_____

REFRAME OR MOVE TO CIRCUMSTANTIAL

_____
_____
_____

SOMETHING IN YOU HAS TO DIE IN ORDER TO GROW

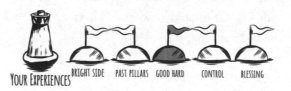

YOUR EXPERIENCES   BRIGHT SIDE   PAST PILLARS   GOOD HARD   CONTROL   BLESSING

As I look at the formative experiences of so many people I admire, story after story illustrates a point that I couldn't understand until I went through a year that felt impossibly hard: our hardest seasons are the ones that allow us to become who we were meant to be. Struggle builds character. Pain produces resolve. Persevering through it and coming out the other side fosters courage. As much as none of us want to have to go through tough times, it's those times that help define who we will become. Consider the following:

- Walt Disney, heralded as one of the world's greatest entertainers, was turned down by 302 banks before getting funding for Disney World.
- Bill Gates's first business failed miserably, a failure he credits for the unparalleled success he experienced at Microsoft.
- President Franklin Roosevelt, broadly considered one of the most important figures in American history, was paralyzed after contracting polio and led the country from a wheelchair.
- Steven Spielberg, the only director to have made more than $10 billion at the box office from his films, was rejected three times from USC's film school.
- Oprah Winfrey, one of the most successful and influential people in the history of media, was born into poverty, endured sexual abuse, and lost an infant child.
- JK Rowling's first *Harry Potter* manuscript was rejected by twelve publishing houses before the series went on to sell more than 500 million copies.
- Michael Jordan was cut from his high school basketball team before he went on to win six championships, five MVP awards, and two Olympic gold medals.
- Thomas Edison failed thousands of times before inventing the light bulb. He was quoted as saying, "I have not failed. I found ten thousand ways that won't work."

In all of these stories, we find recurring themes. An unwillingness to quit when faced with resistance. Reframing failure as an opportunity to learn. Using setbacks as fuel for success. Finding the courage to persevere when critics cast doubt on the quality of their work. I hope that the stories of these incredible people inspire you to ask yourself: *How might the headwinds I am facing be preparing me for what's next?*

The Bible, too, is filled with stories of perseverance and overcoming tall odds. Jonah, Joseph, and Job to name a few. In one of the more famous stories of resilience, a man named Lazarus literally had to die to be brought back to life. In the midst of my own season of transition, that had me asking: *What part of you might have to "die" so that you might be brought back to life? Ego? Status? A relationship? Comfort? Identity? Normalcy?*

I know in my hardest year ever, the storms introduced in my life were catalysts for growth. I got in the best shape of my life, drew closer to my faith, developed deeper relationships with my children, established the most meaningful friendships of my life, and had the opportunity to inventory what mattered (and maybe more important, what didn't) in a way I never had before. Sure, I didn't like that growth had to come the way that it did, but on the other side of benefiting from it, I can find gratitude that my best year ever wasn't a thing that would happen according to my plan. Things in my life had to die—as it turned out, really important things. Grieving those losses and processing that pain took me into places that were a wild departure from my comfort zone. My growth, this evolution of who I'm becoming, didn't happen in spite of these hard things, but because of them.

In this season of growth through pain, I read a book called *When Things Fall Apart* by Pema Chödrön. It's a book that's full of poignant quotes, but this one in particular has stuck with me: "To be fully alive, fully human, and completely awake is to be continually thrown out of the nest. To live fully is to be always in no-man's-land, to experience each moment as completely new and fresh. To live is to be willing to die over and over again."

In a year when I saw my marriage, career, sense of normalcy, and identity all die in some form, I was also forced to rise and create my life anew from the ashes. As Tyler Durden said in *Fight Club*, "It's only after we've lost everything that we're free to do anything." So, 2020, you thought you took me down, but really, you set me free. The sky's the limit.

At the end of my days, when I'm asked about the most important, impactful years of my life, I know beyond a shadow of a doubt that this hardest year ever will be near the top of my list. The man I'll become in the next forty years was born in 2020. That eighty-five-year-old version of me, who will be proud of the impact of his life's work and the way he showed up for himself and the people he loved, will have this incredibly hard season to thank for who he became. That older version of Dave will look back and thank the things that had to die to create his *best year ever*.

LOGBOOK

JOURNALING ACTIVITY

Grab your journal and jot down what comes to you as you reflect on the following questions:

- How have the hard things you've been through created power in you?
- What advantages do you now possess after coming out the other side of your season of struggle?
- What's a word to describe what you've been through that makes you feel brave?

GIVE UP CONTROL

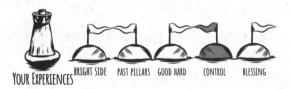

Your Experiences BRIGHT SIDE PAST PILLARS GOOD HARD CONTROL BLESSING

The "illusion of control" is a cognitive bias that leads us to assume that we have control over the outcome of a situation in an instance when we do not. Some part of our humanity needs to believe that we have a say in what happens next. But that need creates weight, anxiety, and a heaviness for the responsibility that comes with having to try to manufacture an outcome that doesn't exclusively depend on our actions. When things don't go our way, the dissonance between what we wanted to happen and what actually happened makes us feel out of control in a way that compromises our courage.

That said, there's freedom in seeing things as they really are. When you think about the experiences that you've had that you didn't expect or see coming, their biggest gifts are often the clarity we're given on how little control we actually have.

Before the diagnosis, the job loss, the unexpected passing of a loved one, the end of a relationship, there may have been a part of us that believed we could make things go our way with enough planning, hard work, manifesting, or prayer. But all of those things presuppose that the universe is operating according to our plan. That our designs are greater than those of a higher power. That's not how life works. Control was never there. Unfortunately, it often takes things falling apart to make that point perfectly clear.

But hear this: Our lack of control isn't a curse. It's a blessing. It's freedom. It's permission to surrender in a way that, as my friend the author and motivational speaker Gabby Bernstein says, "isn't about giving up, but giving over."

Control is an illusion. Anger, regret, frustration for what's happened won't change the past. Worry and anxiety for "what if" or "how long" won't change the future.

The only thing you can control is how you choose to show up today. How you choose to make the most of the hand you've been dealt. How you decide to see the events that led you here as exactly what you needed to grow into who you're becoming. How you resolve to put forth the effort to make the most of every situation, regardless of the circumstance.

Been through a hard time? How is this struggle building a resilience and strength you never imagined?

Feeling rejected by life not turning out to your plan? Were you let down or set free? Rejected or liberated to become a bigger version of yourself?

What would it mean to free yourself from the burden of trying to control what's next? How would the knowledge of your inability to control the future give you permission to fully focus on today? Might you find a capacity for courage over the next twenty-four hours rather than feeling like you have to commit to braving the next twenty-four years and the endless scenarios of what *might* happen?

I highly recommend reading *The Power of Now* by Eckhart Tolle. Tolle's primary hypothesis is that to connect to true peace and a deeper sense of fulfillment, we must be fully present in what we're experiencing in real time. Tolle writes, "Realize deeply that the present moment is all you have. Make the NOW the primary focus of your life." It's a call to action that requires that we work against ego, the part of our being that throws us off track because we're unable to let go of what we've been through, or because we tell ourselves stories about how we'll get the happiness desired *when* . . . when we achieve some goal, or when we get to some level of status, or when we have a certain amount of money in our bank account. *Someday.*

In the end, we have a choice to make. We can allow our ego to continue to tell us the lies about being in control, or we can face the scary and liberating freedom that comes in recognizing that control isn't real. It doesn't exist.

And when things get hairy, find yourself a quiet spot, take a string of deep breaths, and speak the Serenity Prayer out loud:

God, grant me the serenity to accept the things I cannot change,
courage to change the things I can,
and wisdom to know the difference.

We have to decide if we'll continue to let the events from our past or the worry of our future keep a hold on how we move forward in the present, or if we can accept that our past has led us right to where we're supposed to be. In the end, the weight we carry of what the future might hold is unnecessary baggage since we don't have a say in it anyway.

You get this day, today, to do with what you can. What a relief. Here's to taking charge of today. Living fully into the only thing you can control: how you choose to show up in the next twenty-four hours.

LOGBOOK

JOURNALING ACTIVITY

Pull out a piece of paper and make a list of every single thing in your life that is causing you stress and anxiety. Once you have your list, identify the things that you have no control over the outcome of in the next twenty-four hours. Cross them off one by one and see what should be just a handful of things that are left. Now that your list has gone down from fifteen things to around four, can you identify something that previously felt overwhelming but is now suddenly light, manageable, and open for your action?

   For each of the items still left on your list, write down one thing you can commit to doing in the next twenty-four hours to get a step closer to resolution.

   Load lightened. Control given up. Plan created. You got this.

UNANSWERED PRAYERS

There's a famous Garth Brooks song called "Unanswered Prayers" that feels like a fitting way to end our conversation on experiences. The song starts with a real-life story of a man and his wife meeting his old high school flame and his memory of praying for this woman to be his forever. That if he could get just that one thing, he wouldn't ask for anything ever again. At the time, his world, his life, depended on it. As a listener, you understand that this man didn't get what he wanted back then, but that he did end up with the life he was meant to live. In the liner notes of the album, Brooks wrote, "Every time I sing this song, it teaches me the same lesson . . . happiness isn't getting what you want, it's wanting what you've got." Preach.

One night a couple months into my divorce, I was reminded of this song while sitting out back on my patio after putting my daughter, Noah, to bed. Just before heading back inside, I decided to open Facebook, which showed me the "on this day" memory from four years earlier.

Four years ago on that day, Rachel and I had gone to a hospital to pick up newborn twins that we planned to adopt. They would complete our family. We brought them home, named them, and loved them. Then, eight weeks in, we were told of their un-adoptability. The system's misrepresentation of their status meant they'd need to leave our home. We were devastated that the vision for our future was snatched away. Impossibly impossible.

Just as I opened Facebook, a lightning storm started in the distance. As I sat there under a chorus of thunder, I was overwhelmed by the moment, recalling the bedtime routine an hour earlier with Noah, whom we'd adopted after the heartbreak of the twins. A bedtime that included a book and a song and a serious conversation with a small mermaid doll.

If things had gone according to our plans four years earlier, we wouldn't have Noah. One of the brightest and most important lights in my life wouldn't exist. And while I'll pray every day for those babies that came and went, I now recognize that this heartbreak we went through would produce one of the greatest gifts of my life. This serves as a constant reminder to me today that some of the best parts of our lives come from impossible things and unanswered prayers.

The experience on my patio that night offered a profound sense of hope in a dark time. A reminder that in a few years I'd have perspective on how my own unanswered prayers turned into the reason my life became full in a way it was meant to.

If your plan isn't coming together as you'd hoped, I encourage you to believe that there's a Noah-like happy ending on the other side of this struggle even if it's hard to see it in real time. I encourage you to make a deliberate, intentional choice to look for the good that will come at the end of your struggle.

For me, that burst of hope on the back patio began a daily exercise of listing things I was grateful for, even in this time of darkness following my divorce:

The pride of watching my son Jackson slaying his musical theater performance.

The warm embrace of the Field 4 bleachers where I'd cheer on my son Sawyer pitching.

The joy in my son Ford's eyes with his determination to grow a garden out back.

The wonder of my daughter, Noah, embracing preschool and dance and everything else.

The way becoming a godfather for the first time still feels like winning the lottery.

The simple reminder at the local pond that the fish still bite.

The subtly magic moments at dusk out front on bikes that still ride.

The deep gratitude for new friendships that can bloom just as easily in seasons of pain.

The connection that came on an oversized couch each night with the boys and a TV series.

The beauty that bedtimes still include mermaids and songs and an elaborate handshake-hug-kiss combo that only we know.

Not long after that thunderstorm, my parents came to town. They are the absolute greatest. It had been months since I'd seen them, and so much in my life had changed since our last visit. As my dad and I were out on the local golf course one morning, I was reminded of the beauty of the simple, important things that will always exist, like the bond between a father and son. After dinner with my kids that same night, my oldest son asked if I would help him shave. For the first time. Hair on his actual face. Well, lip.

Who knew you could get so emotional showing your spawn how to hold a dang razor? But it's a thing that got me with some serious tears. The timing of this magic shaving cream moment, following a morning on the golf course with my own dad doing a thing we love, reminded me of something I'd forgotten on hard days:

Not only is there already so much good—*there's so much good to come,* especially in being a dad to my kids.

One day I'd be out there on the golf course with them. Or teaching them to drive. Or talking to them about dating other humans with respect. Or showing them how to love again after they get their hearts broken. Or celebrating their individuality. Or drawing them closer to our faith. Or showing them accountability inside unconditional love. And one day, I hope to be the coolest grandpa to their kids. In that moment I could connect to the reality that there was so much beauty ahead. I had a glimpse that the future in front of me would be even more incredible than I'd imagined.

Even if you are going through a tough season, it doesn't take a magical shaving cream moment to recognize this truth: there is so much that's already beautiful in this life, and there's so much more to come. While you may be experiencing a season of grief, I hope you're able to see and feel all the good that still exists. I pray you can keep the faith for the blessing that sits on the other side of not getting what you want. Even as you wade through the storm, remember some of God's greatest gifts are unanswered prayers.

LOGBOOK

JOURNALING ACTIVITY

Make a list of all the good that exists, in spite of the challenges in your life. No matter what's happening in your life right now, take stock of every single thing, big and small, that you have reason to be grateful for today. This practice of being on the lookout for gratitude is a good one to cultivate. Gratitude is an instant catalyst for courage because when you see good in the present, you know that you will see it in the future as well.

OWNING
WHERE YOU ARE

As we kick off this chapter on *where you are,* I want to offer an additional cautionary note about the hubris of believing that we're ever actually in control. That the things we've come to expect are things that can be counted on forever.

The truth is: there is no safe harbor.

There are no guarantees of what tomorrow will bring.

THE DANGER OF SAFE HARBOR

OWNING WHERE NOTHING'S   IT'S ON
YOU ARE   SAFE   YOU

This may sound a little scary, but we are in much better shape to meet the challenges of the future if we give up the illusion of safe harbor. I want you to find the courage and resolve to leave where you are and heed the call that sits beyond the harbor. Even though that call comes at the expense of your comfort. Even though it requires you to let go of the familiar. Burn the altar of what you know for the invitation to something new.

In the debate over taking the chances required to unlock fulfillment, you'll weigh the pros and cons of staying where you are because you believe you know how this version of life unfolds. But that may be counterintuitive because control is an illusion in either place. "In control" describes the person who is moving forward to actively create their destiny rather than waiting for it to be handed to them. Manufacturing their next moves instead of having to react to a move made *to* them. Who really has more control?

Over the years, I have often talked to the teams I work with about the difference between an *incumbent* and an *insurgent* mentality. In business, an incumbent has things going well enough, may even have a large share of the market and steady growth in their sector. But in taking for granted that the steadiness and security they feel will continue into the future, they fail to pay attention to possible disruptors that could derail their success. The insurgent, on the other hand, is making the moves that foster innovation by intentionally looking to disrupt. They push into the spaces that the incumbent wouldn't think of. Untested, uncomfortable spaces where failure thrives, but so does opportunity. The insurgent's hunger for owning their destiny drives their ambition and the courage to try things others don't, to find the breakthroughs others won't.

When I worked in Disney's home video division, Blockbuster Video was an incumbent business that had become a tradition for the home movie-watching experience. The blue marquee on what seemed like every corner was a weekend destination for decades. At the peak of its rental business in 2004, Blockbuster had more than nine thousand stores and was practically printing money. Then along came a company called Netflix, an insurgent that was trying to disrupt the way people enjoyed movies at home.

In contrast to Blockbuster's complacency and comfort with a "harbor" they assumed would always be safe and the company's unwillingness to invest short-term capital into long-term innovation, Netflix was exclusively thinking about how the evolving needs of consumers presented opportunity to leverage technology and offer utility through a seamless supply chain. It was at this height of Blockbuster's business that Netflix made them an offer: you can have our company for $50 million. The insurgent's vision for the future justified a value at the time that was higher than the market called for, but they felt it was warranted given their confidence in the destiny they were creating.

Blockbuster turned the offer down. A little more than a decade later, they were out of business.

Gone in part because the insurgent Netflix was willing to push into unprecedented spaces, an effort that today sees them worth $221 billion, 4,500 times their original offer.

But more pointedly, Blockbuster is gone because of a belief that the owners at the time held that the world they knew would be around forever. That nothing could ever destroy their safe harbor. It's the same hubris that upended Kodak. Even after inventing the digital camera in 1975, the company stood by what they knew in their core film business as others took what could have been their future and ended it. It's the same fate of Toys "R" Us, Tower Records, Pan Am Airlines, Sears, and countless others.

The business lesson of this difference in incumbent versus insurgent mentality has as much application for the aspiring entrepreneur as it does for the person who desires a full life. Clinging to how things are will not keep them as they are. Playing it safe will not guarantee that the harbor you're familiar with will still be intact after unexpected storms make landfall. The surprise diagnosis, reduction of staff at the office, the end of a relationship, or the passing of a loved one all are things that will fundamentally uproot *where you are*.

This isn't an attempt to be a doomsday pessimist. Quite the opposite. I'm trying to light a fire under you, and to offer hope in the idea that your current station in life is not permanent. This can be viewed as both a positive and a negative. Those of us who are willing to explore what lies beyond the jetty will discover new lands, new adventure, and the treasure that awaits.

I want to start this section with a quote from a surprisingly poignant 2014 commencement speech made by actor and comedian Jim Carrey (who is known for many things, though maybe not poignancy). He said:

"My father could have been a great comedian, but he didn't believe that that was possible for him. And so he made a conservative choice. Instead, he got a safe job as an accountant. And when I was twelve years old, he was let go from that safe job and our family had to do whatever we could to survive. I learned many great lessons from my father, not the least of which was that you can fail at what you don't want, so you might as well take a chance on doing what you love."

Action creates opportunity. Taking that action is only possible if we're willing to appreciate that what is will not always be. Here's to letting initiative and insurgency create the opportunities that unlock your purpose. The courage to take a chance on doing what you love.

LOGBOOK

JOURNALING ACTIVITY

Ask yourself: "If I knew that I only had two years left to live, how would I approach my life differently?" Jot down your answers. This was the most important question asked of me as I was summoning the courage to leave my own harbor. Part of what comes in the answer to this question should be leading you toward the life that you should be living, beyond your safe harbor.

YOU ARE THE MIRACLE

OWNING WHERE YOU ARE   NOTHING'S SAFE   IT'S ON YOU

When I was growing up, my grandma would tell this story about a man of faith in a surging flood.

The rain is pouring down, the water around his house rising, and it's getting higher and higher. A big truck comes plowing through and when it gets to his now-submerged driveway, the driver shouts, "Get in!" From his porch, the man declares, "No thank you. I'm a man of faith. I know God will provide." And the truck drives on.

An hour later, as the water continues to rise, it's now breached the house with no signs of stopping. A man in a small boat motors to the now wide-open front door and shouts, "Get in!" Floating on a couch, the man declines: "No thank you. I'm a man of faith. I know God will provide." And the boat floats away.

An hour later, the water has submerged the house. The man is standing on the roof as a helicopter flies low overhead. Over a speaker, the pilot shouts, "Get in!" Standing in ankle-deep water on the roof of his house, the man refuses: "No thank you. I'm a man of faith. I know God will provide." And the helicopter speeds off.

An hour later, the man is dead. Drowned. He gets to heaven and he confronts God in frustration: "God, I have been faithful. I told everyone and anyone that you would provide. Why did you let me drown?" And God looks at him and says, "I sent you a big truck, a small boat, and a helicopter. What more were you looking for?"

Faith alone is not enough. The man needed to act, to take some responsibility to move toward the help and tools that existed and were made available to him to save his life. On this journey into the unknown, yes, you will need faith. Cling to it, rely on it, use it to find courage. But also, you're going to need to act. You're going to need to take responsibility for the work required to stay afloat. It will take effort and action to navigate successfully around the "ship killers" that might slow your journey or sink it altogether.

Start with faith that you will eventually reach the next shore, but don't depend on that faith exclusively. Use your faith as a springboard and then reinforce it with discipline and tapping into your resources and the support of those you trust to help you get where you're going.

There is a passage in the Bible that speaks specifically to my point: "As the body without the spirit is dead, so faith without deeds is dead" (James 2:26).

That said, sometimes believing you have what it takes to perform the necessary tasks, pushing past pride to ask for help, dismissing ego to do the work that's required can be so hard. In my late thirties and early forties, ahead of my career transition away from Disney, I was struggling through a midlife mess, getting in my own way, and not showing up the way my family deserved. I was stuck at the bottom of a ditch, in many ways waiting (faithfully) for the truck, boat, or helicopter to come save me. To pull me out of my funk.

At one of the lowest points, I fell to my knees and threw my hands in the air, yell-talking a prayer: "Please, God! Send me a miracle! Send me the help I need to get out of this mess! Throw a rope into this ditch! Something! Anything! Please!"

And in a way that was clearer than any previous response to prayer, I heard, "Dave, you are the miracle. I've given you all the gifts you could ever need to get out of this mess. They are already present inside you."

The epiphany that I already had what I needed made me believe that I did. It made me brave amidst my fear. It's a choice that you'll need to make if you're going to succeed in this journey. Faith isn't just about the promise of the shore, but also faith in yourself as the captain, fully equipped and capable of getting yourself there.

That by no means suggests that you'll do it alone. When I felt this call to take action, much of that action brought a cast of supporters around me to facilitate my momentum. The couch of a therapist, the circle of a mastermind, the authors of books, the breakthroughs at conferences, the accountability of my closest friends and family and the community with a God who helped remind me of what I'm capable of so long as I act.

In this pursuit of becoming, look for the small miracles that will be afforded to every single one of us in the midst of crossing the ocean. Maintaining a self-awareness of where you are and what you need to successfully push through inevitable obstacles will help inoculate you from the distractions of pride, ego, or blind faith.

Do you believe that you are already enough, worthy, and capable of the life you're pursuing? You'll have to believe it if you're going to reach the vision of the life to which you aspire and the person you hope to grow into. Owning where you are starts by confronting the spaces where you question your worthiness or capabilities. It takes work to reframe those beliefs or reinforce your toolbox to fortify you with the things you need to create certainty in being completely qualified for this pursuit.

Are you willing to be honest about the areas where you struggle? This book is an attempt to help you map the journey from where you are to where you're going and what it's going to take to get there. But if you can't be honest about where you currently are because of guilt or shame or stigma or pride, it will be for nothing.

Struggle thrives in the dark. It festers and grows until it undermines our confidence, compromises our motivation, and obliterates our courage. Your struggle is not a sign of weakness, it's a reflection of your humanity. I struggle, you struggle, everyone struggles. But only the people who are willing to be extraordinarily honest in addressing those struggles will be able to overcome and move past them. Only in that honesty can you develop a plan to get to where you deserve to be.

Are you willing to get the help you need? It could be accepting the offer of assistance when provided in a flood. It could be the willingness to ask for help when it's needed, or pushing past the shame associated with needing it in the first place. Or some combination of all three. Asking for help is one of the most courageous things you could ever do. You will never get help if you turn it down when it's offered. And you will never reach your destination without help. So if you have any resistance to the notion of "help," part of owning where you are requires that you deconstruct those barriers to allow you a fighting chance in the journey ahead.

Hear this: You are the miracle. The gifts you'll need in this push beyond your comfort zone are present inside you already. Some are more fully formed and just need to be believed in, by you. Others are like seeds, waiting for you to water them with the readily available resources and support that will fully bring them to life.

If you are feeling stuck, as I was, waiting at the bottom of a ditch for someone to throw you a rope, I urge you to recognize this important truth: no one is coming to save you. You have to save yourself. It starts with taking an honest look in the mirror. Once you acknowledge where you are, with unflinching honesty, you will truly be able to take the action, ask for help, and do the work to activate the miracle inside you. Let's go.

LOGBOOK

JOURNALING ACTIVITY

It's mantra time. Don't roll your eyes at me. My daughter has a daily mantra that reminds her that she's the miracle every morning:

I am smart.

I am strong.

I am brave.

I can do anything,

and I love myself.

What are your five short statements that declare who you are? Write them down, put them up on your mirror, and get in the habit of saying them out loud like you mean it every day.

SECTION 2
WHERE YOU ARE GOING

BUILDING
A PLAN

B efore setting sail, every good captain runs through a pre-departure checklist to ensure they're prepared for the journey ahead. A good list starts with the basics like flotation devices, first-aid kits, a GPS locator, and the right set of maps and charts to safely and effectively navigate the seas ahead. Next, they work through the equipment that fortifies the ship's seaworthiness: the fuel and oil, the bilge and pumps, lights and batteries required to successfully make the voyage. And finally, there's the list of contingencies to consider should things not go to plan: the weather, a float plan that keeps people on land aware of where you should be, a surplus of water and clothes just in case.

WHAT DO YOU NEED IN THIS SEASON?

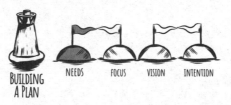

BUILDING A PLAN NEEDS FOCUS VISION INTENTION

In the simplest terms, as you contemplate where you are going, it really comes down to just three important things:

1. *A radically honest assessment of where you are.* It's time to do a deep audit of what's working and what isn't in your life today. How are you currently organizing your day to set yourself up for success? Where are the barriers to your pursuit? This deep audit will include:

   > *Assessing the effectiveness of your existing habits and routines.*

   > *Examining the way your current coping mechanisms prepare you to handle the headwinds in the journey ahead.*

   > *Reviewing your calendar over the past twelve months to see where you've gotten a good return on time invested and maintained the right kind of boundaries.*

   > *Taking stock of the circle of people who influence you.*

   > *Considering whether the media and content you consume (who you follow on social media, how much news you watch, how many hours you dedicate to screens) is consistent with your personal values and the vision for where you want to go.*

   > *And the work we've started in the beginning of this book around your calling, values, identity, and experiences.*

2. *A very clear, specific, detailed vision of where you'd like to go.* This is the work of this section of the book and the detail that we'll unpack in the coming chapters, but the most critical piece here is understanding that unless you know where you're going, you have no chance of getting there. So, it's going to take:

   > *A vision of who you'll become that runs like a movie in your head.*

   > *A plan for how you'll regularly show up, aligned with your personal values.*

   > *A detailed description of the kind of lifestyle you want to experience every day.*

An ability to turn limiting beliefs into empowering beliefs that support why you're qualified for where you're headed.

3. *The tactical details required to get you from here to there.* These are the specifics that this book finishes with. Once we know where we're going, we unpack how we'll get there. Diving into:

How to build the habits and routines you'll need to commit to daily.

Hacking your motivation to maintain momentum on the days you don't feel like it.

Reframing failure as the price of entry for the growth journey you're on.

Building the confidence and emotional intelligence to allow you to succeed.

Understanding the kind of support necessary to hit that shore.

As much as we're going to dive into these three steps in helping build out your plan, just like the captain of a boat, the consideration for how you engineer the life you desire requires a pre-departure checklist. A focus on the fundamentals that must be addressed before you can even contemplate leaving the harbor.

In my journey of becoming, I've had to ask a single foundational question that allows me to entertain any of it:

What do I need in this season?

If I'm going to build a plan for my future, how do I make sure that I'm operating from a stable base that allows me to move forward? I have established a sense of stability surrounding the five dimensions of my health: mental, emotional, physical, spiritual, and relational. Creating this stability acts as a catalyst for courage. It enables me to maintain equilibrium when the ship starts rocking.

LOGBOOK

JOURNALING ACTIVITY

Take time to write out in as vivid detail as possible the vision of where you're headed five years from now. Get as specific as possible about every element. Write as much as you can for as long as you can until that visual becomes a thing that you can see like a motion picture running in your head.

MY PRE-DEPARTURE CHECKLIST

Moving toward my vision of who I am becoming starts with answering this question: What do I need in this season that will allow me to work toward the vision of who I hope to become?

What follows is my Pre-Departure Checklist. These are the items that I need and the actions I must undertake to prepare myself for and fuel myself throughout this journey. Your list will of course be different from mine, and you will want to tailor your personal checklist items as needed.

What do I need in this season to support my *physical health*?

- *Fuel my body with foods that bless it.* Understanding which foods give me the energy for the day I want to have and which foods make me feel the way I want to feel while avoiding the things that don't suit me or my interest in forward motion. For me that includes more greens, lots of protein, fewer carbs, and no booze.
- *Move my body to change the way I think.* Most of my physical goals are connected to my mental health as well. I get out and move every single day for at least thirty minutes, but usually for an hour because of the way my road work has been a fantastic combination of therapy and church.

- *Set aggressive goals to remind myself of how strong I can be.* I've needed things to work toward that were beyond my previous physical thresholds to show myself that, even in a hard season, I can do hard things. The "Better, Stronger" lesson of a mountain climb was why I set a monthly two-hundred-mile running target after my divorce. And it's why I find myself currently training for my first Iron Man. I can do hard things.

What do I need in this season for my *spiritual health*?

- *I need to connect to a power greater than myself every single day*, especially in a world where things feel more out of control and less predictable than usual. I feel that connection as I sit on a rock after my morning run, as I start my day in prayer, and as I relax on my back patio each night where music connects me to closing the day well.
- *Community with people who share my beliefs* to reinforce and remind me of my truth on the days my faith feels tested. Runs with my pastor, coffee with a friend from church, conversations about life and perspective over barbecue out back.
- *Diverse points of view that broaden my understanding and appreciation of God*, the universe, nature, energy, and how all are interconnected in this experience of life. In a season of struggle, I found a connection to all of them in the most unexpected and beautiful places.

What do I need in this season for my *emotional health*?

- *I need to find ways to understand what I'm feeling and why I'm feeling it.* My answer in a hard season has been investing time and energy in reading books that might help me through my grief and the pain that comes in a transitioning family. Recently I've been spending time each night with Michael Singer's *Untethered Soul*, Joe Dispenza's *Evolve Your Brain*, Donald Miller's book on relationships and intimacy called *Scary Close*, and Don Miguel Ruiz's practical guide to personal freedom, *The Four Agreements*, along with the aforementioned

Eckhart Tolle's *The Power of Now* and Pema Chödrön's *When Things Fall Apart*.

- *I need some dang peace.* Yes, it's part of my practice on the back patio once the kids are down, or gone, but also, for the first time in my life, I've been meditating to help bring myself back to neutral when things start to spin.
- *I need to stay connected to all that I have to be grateful for.* All the good in my life. When we take on a challenge, it can be so easy for our focus to train on the hard, so it takes intentionality and commitment to looking for the good, writing it down, and being on the hunt for it all day. If you go looking for it, you will find evidence of it everywhere.

What do I need in this season for my *mental health*?

- *Professional freaking help.* I've never been so serious about the importance of talking through the feeling of choppy waters with an objective person who can provide you the opportunity to normalize your struggle and ask questions about how you might reframe your experience.
- *Purpose, meaning, and impact from the work I do going forward.* As I cast the vision for what my future looks like, I'm crafting through a framework that considers what I stand for (personal values), who I'm trying to become (my "personal brand" for lack of a better term), and the tools I can create to afford the full use of my gifts for maximum impact.
- *Grace.* I need a huge serving of grace when I push into new spaces. Appreciating the nonlinear nature of the pursuit for more has been hard but important. As we collectively experience the motion of the ocean, we have to find ways to appreciate that hard days are just an inevitable part of the human experience and if we have one, it doesn't make us bad or weak or not enough; it makes us normal and regular and human.

What do I need in this season for my *relational health*?

- *Connection.* Sailing into new territory can feel disarming, scary, and at times lonely. People might not understand your decisions to deviate from who you've been for who you're becoming. Finding community with people who share your passion and openness to vulnerability makes the voyage manageable.

- *I need to lean into my family.* The only way I can pursue the impact I hope for in the future is by staying connected to what's most important to me, the glass balls that can't drop. My four kids and a strong co-parenting relationship act as fuel when the pursuit gets hard. For me, it means meeting my kids where they are, fighting for conversation and eye contact free from devices while creating consistency in what are now two homes.

- *Boundaries from anyone who wants to steal my fight for joy.* My calendar, social feed, and text exchanges are all exclusive to positivity. Life is already hard enough to have to also carry the weight of a jerk. Part of my routine is regularly auditing how the things I consume and the people I interact with make me feel.

What's on your pre-departure checklist? What do you need in this season across these five dimensions of health to prepare you for the journey ahead?

LOGBOOK

JOURNALING ACTIVITY

Make your own pre-departure checklist around the five dimensions of health. What do you need in this season for your physical, mental, emotional, relational, and spiritual health? Consider up to three things for each dimension that, were you to commit to them, might propel you closer to who you're hoping to become in the journey.

THE LIGHTHOUSE

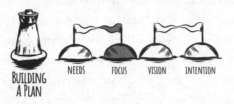

BUILDING A PLAN

NEEDS   FOCUS   VISION   INTENTION

In the earliest days of seafaring, before advanced navigational systems and effectively defined ports, a ship approaching its destination would be guided by a lighthouse. The elevated beacon designed to broadcast light through an evolution over time of fire, lamps, and lenses that acted as the directional aid. No matter the length of the journey, size of the swells, or the strength of the winds, a constant for any sailor was the promise that when they approached land there would be a light to guide them.

As time went by, lighthouses increasingly also came to signal the treacherous parts of the sea. The reefs and rock, jagged coastlines, and promontories that could sink a ship.

In either case, keeping eyes fixed on the lighthouse was essential to any captain's ambition in reaching their destination. Training their focus on where they were headed, what might get in the way, and nothing else. Keeping an eye on the lighthouse came to define what really mattered most in getting home.

As we contemplate how to build our plan and construct the map of where we're headed, it will require the same kind of focus on what really matters, and maybe more important, what doesn't matter at all. We'll need to construct our own lighthouses to draw constant attention to our destination and continually keep us aware of the dangers that might sink us along the way.

Create a Plan

Another important read for me this past year was a book called *Essentialism* by Greg McKeown, a study in what really matters, and what doesn't matter at all, in our lives. In it, he dives into the importance of deliberately distinguishing the *vital few* from the *trivial many*. In a world that tries to tell us to be all things to all people at all times, it's crucial to realize that if everything matters then nothing matters. That if everyone is important, then no one is truly important. That as much as we'd like to make a list of our top priorities, there is no such thing as "top priorities"; only one thing can be a priority at one time.

My takeaway? The mandate for effectively building a plan becomes a deliberate and intentional focus on the needle movers. Doing the work to stay connected to your core values the way you'd hope to experience life on a day-to-day basis, and saying yes *only* to the things that support them, and a polite but firm *no* to everything else. And I do mean everything.

Focusing only on the things that matter and releasing everything else that doesn't is an act of cultivating courage. When you know that the things in which you're investing your time, energy, brain power, and resources are propelling you to who you hope to become, it catalyzes the bravery required to get there.

Building a plan for the future starts with an inventory of what is truly essential in your life, and eliminating the nonessentials. Creating the guardrails that you'll have to stay inside of if you're going to reach your destination.

The beacon in the distance that reminds you every day where you're going, and the things you'll need to consistently avoid to get there safely.

One of my favorite lines from *Essentialism* is, "If you don't prioritize your life, someone else will." Their needs filling your calendar at the expense of your self-care, the goals you've set, the destination you're heading toward. Their comfort being catered to at the expense of your fulfillment. Their expectations having you question what you expect from yourself.

McKeown argues that there are three core truths to which you need to connect if you hope to successfully focus on your own list of essentials:

- *"I choose to."* You are the captain of your ship. The owner of your calendar. The person who gets to decide how the actions you take and the things you commit yourself to align with your values and set you up to reach your destination. It requires reframing the way you think of self-care (it is not selfish but a requirement for successfully navigating the journey while showing up well for those we love). It forces connecting the pursuit of your goals to honoring the purpose that was put in you by your creator in a way that doesn't make you feel bad for heeding the call. When you become comfortable making other people uncomfortable (and you will) in the move from "I have to" to "I choose to," you'll have the freedom to stay focused on your destination.
- *"Only a few things really matter."* A dogged, conscientious, daily return to the vital few. It's the active intentionality to create a calendar, daily routine, and a stream of to-dos that exclusively push you closer to the destination you're heading toward. Asking that big question that entrepreneur and bestselling author Gary Keller does in *The One Thing*: "What's the *one* thing I can do such that by doing it everything else will be easier or unnecessary?" Those are the things to say "yes" to. These are the things to fill your calendar with and train your focus on.
- *"I can do anything but not everything."* Playing against the impossibly high societal standard that we should be able to do all things (and have it all together while we attempt to) truly

only guarantees one thing: you will not do any of those things particularly well. Your effort and impact will be diluted across a spectrum of things that inherently have varying degrees of value, and the time *wasted* on low-value to-dos absolutely compromises the quality of those things that really do matter. These are the things connected to your values, that light your heart on fire. That enable you to be the light bearer you were intended to be. That are connected to progress and momentum in your journey.

When you make a decision to leave something familiar for something unknown, you will confront a few inevitabilities: when it starts to get scary, you will feel a temptation to come back to what you've known. As you're triggered by the worry of how unstable it feels in these new, uncharted waters, the pangs of impostor syndrome (*might I be found out for not yet knowing how to handle these swells?*) and the insecurity that comes from the guarantee of failure in doing first-time things, will have you consider returning to the normal that you knew. After all, a retreat to the suffering you were familiar with promises something you can count on.

Resist that temptation. Your lighthouse isn't standing on that shore you left. It sits in front you, calling you home. Rather than returning to a normal you knew, a normal that was familiar but unfulfilling, I want to challenge you with this question: *In the rush to return to normal, can you use this time to consider which parts of normal are worth rushing back to?* Is there a possibility that building this plan, that taking this journey of "becoming" might afford you the opportunity to home in on what actually matters and be free from everything that doesn't? Connecting with the very few essentials in your life will give you the freedom to reach your destination faster, more effectively, with more impact, every single time.

Before we move off lighthouses and get after building our plan, there's one more thing to consider about this beacon and its analogy. As much as the lighthouse itself doesn't move, the way the lenses and light are used changes over time. The focal length of the lens can change the refracting power, casting more or less light depending on conditions. The use of tint and color can be used to signal specific kinds of danger. Some lights come on or off based on tide. Most come on and off based on time of day. The bottom line is that as much as the lighthouse itself is a static symbol, a stable declaration of where the next harbor is located, it also uses its light in different ways to help guide people home. A duality of being both immovable and flexible.

As you build a plan, knowing where you're going, the lighthouse on the opposite shore is likely a thing that will not materially change along the way. But the way that the light guides you home, the route you'll take, the things required to get you there will be constantly evolving in the midst of the journey. Your ability to stay focused on what matters, releasing yourself from what doesn't, and keeping an open mind as you navigate: that's what will get you home.

LOGBOOK

JOURNALING ACTIVITY

Start a "what really matters" list. Add to it over time. Audit it over time. When new opportunity presents itself, cross-reference the list to see if it aligns with the things you've determine really matter in your life. When you get an invitation to dedicate time on your calendar to someone else's agenda, consider your answer with a quick check of how it's congruent with your list.

THE POWER OF IMAGINATION

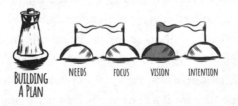

BUILDING A PLAN   NEEDS   FOCUS   VISION   INTENTION

Whether it was life after a failed adoption, the end of my run at Disney, or going through a divorce, one of the biggest challenges for me in the earliest days after each was imagining what my life would look like now that everything had changed. I'd had one vision for how the rest of my life would unfold. But now my plans and dreams for what would come were different, compromising my ability to see an alternative at times that could feel as rich, hopeful, and comfortable as the one I'd been connected to for so much of my life.

As I've mentioned, sometimes the decision to leave a harbor is one you make for yourself, and other times it is made for you. No matter the reason for shoving off, having a vision for where you are going can be the hardest part.

If you are struggling to create that motion picture in your head that gets you fired up, out of bed early, and excited for the work that comes in the pursuit, it may be that you're having trouble separating the circumstances of your present from the possibilities of your future.

I know that was the case for me. As I stood on the dock, one foot in the boat, the chaos of my current situation blurred the imagination for all the good that sat in front of me. The new dreams, deeper relationships, professional pursuits unlocking my calling, those things were clouded by my short-term experience of chaos.

Believing in the version of the coming year I deserved and the kind of life that would unfold for me began with learning to reframe the circumstances of my present in a way that created hope. Hope that exists irrespective of, or maybe even because of the events unfolding in real time.

What you're going through as you build this plan isn't an indicator of what you deserve. What you've experienced isn't a limit for what's possible in this journey ahead. It requires reframing what you're going through into empowering stories of perseverance and strength. Creating a map that unleashes your full potential starts with reconnecting with who you are and why you're here.

For me, jump-starting my imagination came from the community of close friends who helped remind me of who I am deep down. Getting closer to a higher power gave me perspective on what was happening and reminded me that my external circumstances and the essence of my being were in no way connected and never had been. Reading the books on mindset, listening to the podcasts for personal development, immersing myself in the motivational and inspirational content acted as a jumper cable to a battery in need of a charge. It was the invigoration from this combination of sources that would bring me back to the bigger-than-life imagination I had when I was a kid. An imagination that would act as an accomplice in manufacturing courage.

If you find yourself struggling in any way with your vision of the future, ask some questions to understand why:

What's in the way of my imagination?

What did I believe about myself before I was told what to believe about myself?

Who did I want to be before I became who I am?

What's the cost of allowing my dreams to be chipped away over time?

How will I feel if I don't fight to honor what my intuition is already telling me?

That voice inside you knows your passions and has insight into your dreams. Listen to it. Trust that it's there for a reason. Denying the nudge that keeps beating inside you can only end in regret. Don't let that happen. Leverage the fear of regret to kick-start action.

Palliative care nurse turned author Bronnie Ware has written about her experiences with people who were nearing death. In her book *The Top Five Regrets of the Dying*, the single most common regret she heard expressed by those near death was: "I wish I'd had the courage to live a life true to myself, not the life others expected of me."

In her work, Ware recounts how often people realize in the end that many of their dreams have been left unfulfilled. Knowing that their dreams are dying with them, they feel regret for what could have been, for the choices they didn't make, the chances they didn't take, and the times they let other people and the circumstances of life talk them out of imagination.

Hear this: every single great thing in your life sits on the other side of the struggle you find yourself in, on the other side of building a plan so full of imagination that it wakes you up in the middle of the night giddy. It doesn't mean it will be easy, without fear, and without the risk of failure. But it's there if you believe it is.

It starts with imagination. The permission to dream audaciously. The desire to end your life with a look back at how many uncomfortable steps you took before you finally walked in the shoes that were true to your life and its calling. The belief that no matter what you've been through, you are here for reasons worthy of grandiose, abundant, possibly-obnoxious-to-others plans. The purpose of a creator who knows how much light you can afford and who already believes in your ability to deliver it, if you're willing to believe that you can.

LOGBOOK

JOURNALING ACTIVITY

Imagine that you are on your deathbed. You have lived a good, long, full life. A life draped in the courage to boldly step toward fear. I want this ninety-six-year-old future version of yourself to write a letter to you now, listing the things in your life that they are most proud of. Now allow this older, wiser version of you to give you the courage to untie your ropes and push off from the dock.

INTENTIONALITY

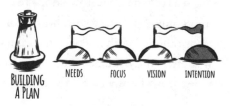

Casting a vision for my future came through a framework I created to help me answer a specific and simple question:

What does your week look like?

I mean, yes, I wrote out a very specific and very detailed version of who I hope to be five years from now, something I hope you did earlier in the book. But I also needed to get into the intricacies of what a normal Monday through Friday would look and feel like between now and then. I started with that five-years-from-now vision, and then did the work of understanding what pieces need to be built over time to make that vision possible.

The vision for your future does in fact need to be something that you can see like a motion picture in your head; the clearer the destination, the easier it will be to plot your course. While connecting to who you'll be years from now is important for guiding the broader direction, it's just as important to create a visualization for how you'll need to show up in the shorter term to make it happen.

Those short-term micro-steps that lead to your long-term goal are the pieces that make up a plan. Your vision for the future includes two crucial ideas:

- A long-term vision. Place the lighthouse you're sailing to in the distance.
- Short-term specifics. Identify the individual buoys that help guide you along the way.

Once you have that sense of what you aspire your week to look like, you get to dive into the specifics. What needs to happen to get you to where you want to be? What needs to be true to turn it from a dream into a reality?

My planning has been as much about how I hope to experience the day as it is about where I'm going. So, I start with how I hope to feel and the way my lifestyle hopes are aligned with my personal values. From there, it's a question of how my personal passion, competencies, and ability to impact others and provide for my family reveal the direction I need to take.

Question 1: What do you stand for?

The first set of guardrails is formed around your personal values. *What do your values ask of you?* The things you must honor in anything and everything you dream up. Knowing your values tells you as much about what you can dream as what you can't. For example, with a value like *work to live, don't live to work*, I know immediately that any project with extraordinary hours or any job opportunity that requires lengthy travel and comes at the expense of being an involved dad is off the table.

Question 2: Who do you want to be?

The second set of gates are around the convergence of the components of my "why." These are the questions of purpose and calling: What do I have passion for, skills around, an opportunity for impact through, and the chance to provide for my family with? The answers inevitably become something of a personal brand. The reputation by which I am known or the way I might be described by someone else who's witnessed my week.

For me there are four pillars: Parenting, Personal Development, Business and Leadership, and Health and Fitness. These are the spaces inside of which I want to play. Any opportunity that aligns with my personal values and also sits inside one of these categories is fair game in my pursuit. It also means that any opportunity to immerse myself in tools or resources that help strengthen my depth of knowledge in these categories is one to actively pursue.

Question 3: How can you use your gifts?

As we've eliminated anything that falls outside of your core values and zeroed in on the industries, business sectors, or (especially if you're building a plan not dependent on finances) personal passions in the areas of who you hope to be, the pool of possibilities has narrowed. Now we can get more specific about how and where your skills and gifts can be applied.

This is the chance to brainstorm anything and everything that you could push toward in the shortest term that has an opportunity to act as a building block to the place you hope to land five years from now. You aspire to be a published writer? Your work here is to consider a creative writing class, a webinar on how to write a book, actually getting words on a page, creating relationships with an agent, or submitting to a publisher, depending on where you are in the process.

Question 4: What's the immediate plan?

Now it's time to set some goals around what we've brainstormed. It's time to prioritize the actions that will make the rest of our tasks easier or allow us to get to our destination faster. In our example of writing a book, this is where you're setting specific goals around each of the individual components necessary to get that baby published. These are detailed short-term goals that create the accountability and momentum to help you reach your destination. Which writing class are you going to take on what days? How many words a day are you going to commit to writing? And so on.

I'm a fan of good old third-grade SMART goals. If you understand how you can use your gifts, then you should be able to see the opportunities that sit in front of you. Now it's time to create a concrete plan for each of your building blocks. You want your plan to be:

- Specific: clearly stated, with a narrow set of details, identify the goal.
- Measurable: develop a way you will track your progress as you go.
- Achievable: setting reasonable goals considering your resources, skills, and time.
- Relevant: goals that align with your personal values and long-term mission.
- Time-based: realistic delivery to motivate and prioritize relative to other goals.

The hope with this framework is that it adds some intentionality to the map that you're drawing. Being intentional in the design of what's next is another ingredient in cultivating the courage that's required to act on the plan once it's in place. A vision that considers what you stand for, who you want to be, how to use your gifts, and what you need to do next. It's a process that requires you to have a clear sense of where you want to be five years from now, but helps you get there by identifying the steps you'll need to take now and every day between now and then to get there. Draw that map and you'll be ready to set sail.

LOGBOOK

JOURNALING ACTIVITY

Roll up your sleeves and work through the framework. It's likely not something that you'll build in one sitting, but I'd encourage you to break from your day-to-day and carve out the time to consider the intended outcome of what you're building. Getting this up-front piece well thought through is worthy of setting aside a full day, possibly with a trusted friend or mentor, to get specific about:

- What you stand for.
- Who you hope to be.
- How you can use your gifts.
- The short-term goals required to get you closer to your long-term vision.

Good luck. This is where it starts getting exciting.

CONFRONTING
YOUR FEAR

F ear is going to be the single biggest threat to your ambition for a better life. Fear of the unknown, fear of what other people will think, fear of failure, fear of not being worthy or ready for the audacity of your vision. Any and all of these versions of fear will arise on your journey. It's a guarantee.

DEAR FEAR

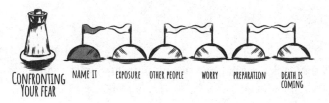

CONFRONTING YOUR FEAR   NAME IT   EXPOSURE   OTHER PEOPLE   WORRY   PREPARATION   DEATH IS COMING

The first thing you need to do is to normalize fear. Recognize that fear is a normal, healthy emotion. Your fear does not mean that you are unique. It does not make you weak or less than. It makes you human and just like every other person who's ever decided to push into something new. Your fear, like mine, was programmed into you. Confronting it and unraveling it, while challenging, is something that you can absolutely do.

With that said, becoming courageous does not eliminate fear. Moments of this journey will still be hairy, scary, and absolutely triggering to those parts of you that want to maintain the status quo. Courage, then, is the single most important tool in allowing us to move forward through the fears that will be even more present as we choose discomfort. Our fears aren't going away; we're just going to equip ourselves with the tools to eliminate those that are lies, be prepared for those that are real, and embody the wherewithal to do it scared on the days they rear their head.

Ironically, just days after finalizing our divorce, I was given some insight on working through my fear by my ex-wife, through an interview she did with author Elizabeth Gilbert. In their conversation they talked about the idea of allowing your fear to write a letter to you when you find yourself on the cusp of doing something creative, new, or bold. Developing the imagination for my new future felt creative, new, and bold, along with a host of not disclosed, expletive-laden descriptors that were all connected to fear. So, letter writing it was.

I sat outside with my spiral-bound notebook, and through a steady stream of tears I wrote a letter to myself from my fear. I made a list of everything I could think of that scared me about developing a plan to reframe my identity, redefining what I'd do for work, understanding what it would mean to be a single parent, and all the rest. When I was done, I had detailed forty-six things that I was afraid of. That's a lot of fear. Here's a bit of my letter (though I have spared you the full forty-six):

Dear Dave,

I am your fear, and this is what I want to tell you. I am afraid . . .

Of the blank piece of paper that sits in front of us in a world where what you thought our life would be is now gone.

Of what it will mean to be fully and totally responsible in a world where you've always had a person that helped you be responsible.

Of doing this without turning to the usual vices to deal with your anxiety, fear, and insecurity.

Of what shedding your identity as a husband means.

Of being alone, growing old alone.

Of how well we can be what the kids need in this choice.

Of starting over and getting it "wrong."

Of putting ourselves out there and failing.

Of your ability to truly love yourself.

Of letting go of what was, for what will be.

That there's something about you that doesn't work right, that at its core doesn't give you happiness or peace or fulfillment that others have access to.

Of being rejected if you show your true self to others.

That the ways you've tried to be what others wanted or needed at the expense of knowing the real you will be an impossible habit to break.

That your wiring to achieve, to be seen as lovable, will always have you trying to convince others that you are.

That you won't find someone who loves you, all of you, flaws and all, unconditionally.

That you don't have the discipline to show up as you could or should.

That you won't learn everything this experience is meant to teach you.

That you'll let the kids down.

That you'll let yourself down.

Of how long it will take to not wake up every morning with this divorce as the first thought of the day.

Of our empty house when the kids aren't here.

Of being forty-five and waking up at sixty to wonder what the heck happened to your life.

Of always being connected to the regrets of "what if."

Of the imagination required to build your future.

That you won't be able to forgive yourself for the role you played in getting us here.

That you'll get stuck.

That even though everyone says it will be okay, it won't.

Sincerely,

Your fear

Good times. I don't say that facetiously. It was a miraculous sigh of re-lief and an incredible boost to my confidence. By bringing these paralyzing insecurities out of the darkness of my unconscious and into the light of my spiral-bound notebook, it allowed me to dismantle the fear that might have held me back from moving forward. It accomplished that by doing two incredibly liberating things:

- *Question which of these fears were real.* Most of us have heard the suggestion that fear is **F**alse **E**vidence **A**ppearing **R**eal. For me, that's exactly what it was. In going line by line, I discovered that many of the things I thought I was afraid of were simply ridiculous. When I started poking at them, the honest interrogation revealed that a good 80 percent of what I'd written down could immediately be eliminated from the list. Be free.
- *Create a plan to address any warranted fear.* I'm not one who believes that all fear is false evidence. I'm never going to get over my fear of getting sick when out to sea. That's a very real fear that anyone traveling with me should take seriously. When it comes to other very real fears, like my fear of failing, you have to follow the line of questions that this feeling prompts. How can you best prepare to *do it scared*? How can you become ready to take this fear on? The ability to formulate the habits and routines, the circle of support, the resources you will need to ready yourself to do it scared will fundamentally change the way you feel about the challenge.

Your fear, like so much of your struggle, thrives in the dark. Getting to know my fear, bringing it into the light, sharing it with the closest people in my life, allowed me to dismantle it. It gave me the opportunity to plan around it. It freed me to conjure the imagination, to take that first step and keep on going when hard times triggered my fears along the way. I know it will do the same for you.

LOGBOOK

JOURNALING ACTIVITY

Write your own letter from your fear. Draw on all of the dark things that are festering inside of you and bring them out into the light. Once you have done this and you have your list of fears, identify which are real and then free yourself from the rest. For the real fears, for-mulate a plan for preparing yourself to face them. This is cultivating courage, in action.

TOE DIP

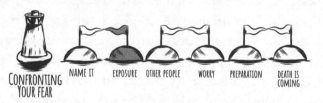

Just before stepping away from the day-to-day of The Hollis Company at the end of 2019, we gathered the leadership team to discuss our vision for where the company was going in the next five years. We were coming off a year that saw success beyond expectation in each division of the company.

There were more than 50 million downloads in our podcast network; the #1 *New York Times* bestselling debut of Rachel's *Girl, Stop Apologizing,* bumping her previous *Girl, Wash Your Face* from the top spot; the immi-nent launch of my first book, *Get Out of Your Own Way,* poised to debut on the list; a clothing line on QVC; a product launch at Target; the sold-out stadium events for RISE; a daily show launching on a streaming platform; a coaching business affording thousands transformation; and a successful direct-to-consumer products operation hitting its stride.

It was a very good year.

Impact and community on a scale we couldn't have possibly imagined. The kind of success that can play tricks with your mind.

As we sat in that conference room with the wind in our sails, the vision for where the company was heading went beyond audacious. Rachel cast the vision for the expansion of partnerships, our charitable foundation, retail destinations, new film and television projects, and more. There was a buzz in the room and a palpable excitement for the work that lay ahead.

Without missing a beat, in a respectful but direct way, I told the room, "No one here has the skills to have a seat at the executive table of this company five years from now. That goes as much for me as it does for all of you. The scale of what we're talking about, the intricacies of what's involved, goes beyond what any of us currently know how to do."

Buzzkill.

And also true.

The reality was that new skills would need to be developed for every one of these talented specialists if they were to be qualified for the ambitious work we were envisioning. A deeper knowledge was required, a broader spectrum of competencies added to an already sturdy foundation. It would require that they push themselves into new spaces to learn new things. It came with a mandate that they face their insecurities, overcome their fear of failing in arenas where they hadn't previously played, and develop the more sophisticated set of prerequisites that the invitation to the boardroom of the future demanded.

The same is true for you.

While you are entitled to every audacious detail of the vision you're casting, when you're dreaming as big as I hope you are, it's unlikely that you currently have the skills, mindset, confidence, habits, emotional intelligence, and experience to get a seat at the head of the table. That doesn't mean you're not good; it doesn't mean you can't get there. Trust me, I don't yet have the ingredients needed to succeed in my five-year vision because I'm a big dreamer like you.

The only way you or I will have what it takes is if we're willing to face the fears that come in the pursuit of new things.

In medicine, inoculation is when you inject a small dose of disease into the body so that the body creates antibodies to fight off that disease. You intentionally take the thing you're trying to protect yourself from, so that the body does it for you.

Fear is a form of disease.

Creating protection from it requires a similar approach.

Though I mentioned I didn't grow up a runner, I now classify myself as one. In an attempt to find more productive coping mechanisms when life gets hard, I put on my shoes. Last year I ran just more than two thousand miles. It was a *hard* year. But getting to a place where I could put up that kind of distance was something that was built over time. It required me to reframe my belief in my ability to have a two-hundred-mile month by slowly exposing myself to longer distances and more strenuous challenges.

Around the same time that the executive team was meeting to talk about the next five years, I found myself climbing a mountain. A thirty-six-hour event called 29029 was the opportunity to replicate the height from the base to the peak of Everest. While I'd never previously climbed a mountain or done anything for literally thirty-six hours straight, I found myself at the base of a Utah mountain ready to see what I could do.

Thirteen climbs up an unbelievably steep incline, at altitude, in the cold, each of which took about an hour and forty-five minutes of the most intense workout of my life. Back to back. Over and over. In what ended up being the most physically and mentally trying day and a half of my life, crossing that finish line rewired me. It reframed what I believed myself to be capable of.

The weekend after the climb, I found myself ready for my weekly "long run." Prior to the mountain, I'd been running about five miles for about an hour's worth of time each Sunday, but on that day, the idea of *only* running for an hour didn't feel "long" anymore. I'd just done thirteen consecutive workouts that were longer than this single jaunt, on flat ground, without altitude, in seventy-four-degree weather. So, I decided I'd run a neighborhood half marathon. Heck, what was 13.1 miles and two and a quarter hours of movement after the weekend I'd just had?

When I finished, I was proud, brimming with confidence for having done something so much greater than what I'd previously believed myself capable of. I decided that it was my new thing. Reframed what my "long run" was. For nineteen consecutive weekends, I ran a half marathon in my neighborhood. On the twentieth weekend, I completed my first marathon in downtown Austin. That afternoon when I got home, floating from the feeling of again having reframed what I now knew I could do, I signed up for my first Iron Man. In showing myself that I could do more than I thought, I thought about how much more I could do.

When our executive team's five-year vision-cast broke, we began meeting with each leader to talk about where they might start their journey of inoculating the fear they had in parts of the business they didn't yet understand. Creating opportunities for those with a fear of public speaking to lead small parts of meetings, those who were overwhelmed by a P/L statement to sit at lunch with our CFO, affording those who didn't like to deliver direct feedback a template for radical, respectful candor.

Acquiring the skills, experience, and mindset to sit at that table in the future required a toe dip into the parts of the business that had previously been overwhelming to them. Building courage one small dose at a time. I hadn't considered myself a marathon runner until my exposure to feats beyond what I believed I was capable of. The same was true for each of them, and it's just as true for you. As you cast your vision and name your fears, the next step is walking right toward them, finding a way to create bursts of small exposure in the hopes of inoculation. It's time to get your feet wet.

LOGBOOK

JOURNALING ACTIVITY

Find one small thing that scares you, and then go do it. Take a drop of that fear. Write down how you feel before you take on that fear. Then write down how you felt after successfully challenging it.

THEM

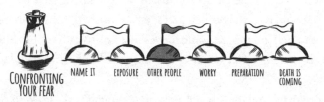

Writing my first book was the proudest accomplishment of my professional life. I'd never worked so hard, been so vulnerable, or wanted something to work more. That last piece, the wanting it to work, played against my greatest fears. *Them.*

Pursuing a life of impact means accepting a journey of criticism. People not liking your work, even hating it, that's the price of entry. In the attempt to serve one hundred people well, you'll upset ten, and so often the human condition has us so concerned with the ten at the expense of serving the ninety. We slow down or don't start at all lest someone decide our light isn't what they were looking for. Here's a gift:

You aren't free ice cream.

You can't make everyone happy. Don't let the critical person for whom your light was never intended keep you from letting it shine for the rest of those who desperately need it. Trust me, there are going to be plenty of people who hate *this* book that I hope you love. That just means this book wasn't written for them. Nevertheless, I'm still so proud of having written it for those it's intended for. I'm giving you the advice I needed to keep writing both books when the voices in my head and the insecurities of my younger self cast doubt on my ability.

I was writing in the shadow of a giant: my wife at the time had two consecutive black swan events in the book world that I both benefited from and was terrified by. Would I be compared to her work? Held to a standard of how well my book sold relative to hers? Would they like my words if they were different from hers? Or think them too similar? What would *they* say? It was paralyzing.

About a week before the book came out, I was given the most incredible gift. A woman from the launch team sent a note saying that her neighbor asked if he could read the book when she was finished. He was interested in a resource to help him make some moves in a positive direction. She shared with me the note he'd left her after finishing the book three days later.

> I want to thank you for this gift. I see some things that I can do to change the way I've been present for my wife and daughters, how I've made room to show up better for myself. Just know that this book will be a turning point for me. —Dean

In a single note from a stranger in Illinois, my book was already a success. My fear of what *they* would think was connected to how much impact it would have, a by-product of my dumb ego. I set out with an audacious ambition to change the world, and I contorted it into needing to touch millions of lives. But I hadn't considered that the world would change if it only touched one. It changed the world of that man, his wife, their daughters, and their circle.

That, in and of itself, is world change.

Don't make my mistake and let the fear of how far your light will shine cause you to hide it because it might not reach enough people. If the YouTube tutorial you create is viewed by one person but that person fundamentally and forever changes the way they can provide for their family, would you create it? If your book brought fifty one-star reviews but kept one person on the verge of taking their life from doing it, would you write it? Talking ourselves out of our dreams because we don't think they'll matter is a lie that keeps us in this suffering we know. Do not believe it.

That said, the fear most people have about *them* isn't over how much impact they'll have, but how much criticism. What they'll say. What they'll think. More games fostered by our ego. The handiwork of our insecurity. If I'm honest, it's an overstated sense of self.

I hate to break this to you, but nobody is thinking about you. They're thinking about themselves.

I dedicated an entire chapter in my first book to this absolutely true fact of life that is so hard for us to get our heads around. This time around, I've decided to break it down in a way we can process to actually set us free. Not worrying about what other people think is a prerequisite for courage. At the end of this chapter, my hope is that you can be liberated from 95 percent of the worry you afford others.

In your life there are three buckets of people:

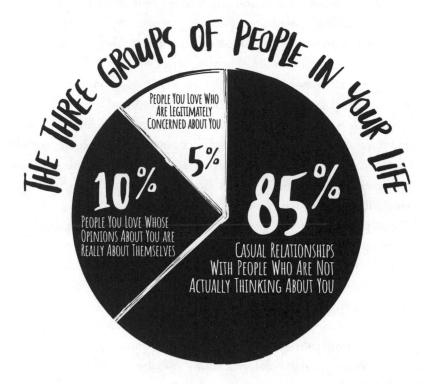

Eighty-five percent are casual acquaintances. These are the people you work with, are friends with online, or you may know from church or a sports team your kid plays on. You know them but you don't do life with them intimately every single day. They know you, too, but you're not calling them when your car breaks down on the side of the road, when you're crying in the bathroom over hard days. These people are not actually *in* your life; they are *around* your life.

These people are not thinking about you, not the way you're worried about. And you're not thinking about them in the way they may be worried about. But even if they *are* thinking about you, their opinions on your life do not matter because they are not *in* your life. They are spectators. You are in the arena. Spectators watch, cheer, and boo, but they do not get a say in how the game is played. Be free.

Ten percent are misguided loved ones. These are people who have opinions that you do care about because you love or crave love from them. When they have thoughts on how you're living your life, it actually has an effect on you. These people, however, are representing their concern for your choices through the lens of their fear, not love. They are giving you advice based on their own limiting beliefs, not the truth of your ability. They mean well, but are misguided because they don't understand your motives, share your values, or appreciate the landscape the way you do.

In my last book I wrote, "If someone does have a problem with something you're doing, it's likely they are challenged by it, feel insecure because of it, are jealous of your willingness to chase after it, or are frustrated that your belief in yourself makes them more aware of their disbelief in their own ability. In the end, it's rarely actually about you."

These people mean well. They are presenting their fear wrapped in love. It's not a gift worthy of accepting because it's not connected to who you are or why you're making this decision. You're following your calling, not theirs. While the intentions of the misguided loved ones are harder to release, they are releasable all the same. Be free.

Five percent are people you love with legitimate concern. These are the people who are in your life, that you love and crave love from, that get your motivation, see the alignment with your values, have some handle on the landscape, and want to engage in a conversation to make sure you're considering every angle. They want to play the role of accountability partner and become an accomplice in your preparation for the journey ahead. You should listen to the opinions of these people.

This doesn't mean that you should *always* do what they say, but being in a community with people who have legitimate concern for you and look to play a role in preparing you for the implications of big decisions is something that all of us need in our lives. No one goes on the journey of self-actualization alone.

In the end, the worry of *them* is one of the biggest anchors that keeps us from making a move in the first place. Our insecurity that our impact won't matter, or that the moves we make might come at the expense of criticism for having taken the step. Remember, the cost of entry for a life of impact is criticism. Even so, most of what you're worried about will never come to pass (they aren't actually thinking about you) or won't matter (they're thinking about things that are disconnected from your values or motives).

What will matter is the difference you can make in a single life when you step into who you were meant to be. This light that sits inside of you is a gift that was meant to be gifted. Shake the worry of what *they* think so you can get busy affecting a lot of *them*.

LOGBOOK

JOURNALING ACTIVITY

Flip to a blank page in your journal and create three columns with "The 85%," "The 10%," and "The 5%" across the top. Think about something you're contemplating. Then place the people whose judgments you're worried about into the three buckets. Spend time with the 5 percent that matter. Release the rest.

MAKE A LIST OF ALL THE AUTHORITY FIGURES YOU'RE WORRIED ABOUT JUDGING YOU AND PUT THEM INTO ONE OF THESE THREE BUCKETS:

SAY GOODBYE TO THESE BUCKETS!

WHAT MIGHT HAPPEN

CONFRONTING YOUR FEAR   NAME IT   EXPOSURE   OTHER PEOPLE   WORRY   PREPARATION   DEATH IS COMING

The ancient Stoic philosophers are known for their wisdom. Names like Marcus Aurelius, Seneca, Epictetus, and dozens of others from two thousand years ago speaking truths that hold up today. While they are known as some of the founders of thought around virtue, ethics, physics, and logic, they also wrestled with the same anxiety that each of us battles with every day.

Anxiety is born out of a perceived fear of what *might* happen, a weight that we've given to the perception of what's possible in a way that disproportionately weights the possibility of worst-case fears coming to pass. Allowing the worries of what might happen to infiltrate our thoughts compromises our confidence, diminishes our courage, and keeps us stuck where we are, paralyzed by fear. (Note: I'm not talking about or trying to diminish clinically diagnosed anxiety disorder, but rather the situational anxiety that keeps us stuck, robs our motivation, and leaves us second-guessing our intuition.)

Epictetus said, "Man is not worried about real problems so much as by his imagined anxieties about real problems." An idea reinforced by Seneca who said, "We suffer more from imagination than from reality." It's a weak spot of our humanity. Allowing our mind to run wild with worst-case scenarios introduces real-time suffering for a reality that has not yet occurred *and likely never will.* Don't allow these mind tricks to upend the pursuit of your calling.

The work with my therapist and the epiphany from *Untethered Soul* about being the observer of your thoughts and emotions come into play here. The more we can disconnect from the worry of what might be and ask why this anxiety is presenting itself, the more likely we are to maintain freedom from the paralyzing impact of the weight that comes in worrying about the future circumstances that *might* unfold that we have absolutely no control over.

Marcus Aurelius said, "Today I escaped anxiety. Or no, I discarded it, because it was within me, in my own perceptions—not outside." Anxiety is the nervousness, worry, apprehension, and fear of things *that have not yet happened.* And because these things have not happened, it also means they might not. Oftentimes the stories we create in our heads are far worse than the actual events that unfold when that thing we're preoccupied with comes to pass.

Case in point: I remember dreading the first night I'd be at home alone post-divorce. In this home where we'd raised our humans and lived as *us,* I created a story about how it would feel once it was down to me, a mini schnauzer named Jeffrey, and a fish named Hawk. The latter two are terrible company. Especially Hawk.

As much as there was consolation in knowing the kids would share time in homes where they would be loved well by both of us as single parents, the images of enduring that first night alone created a narrative in my mind that fueled anxiety, fear, and sadness in the days and weeks prior. The deafening silence. The sadness of setting a single plate for dinner. The bedtime routine that no longer existed. While so many parts of a journey through divorce (or anything hard) are ones where you just have to keep taking steps through a dark part of the forest that you've never been through before, I made the journey much more difficult than it needed to be by holding on to a story of what it would be like before it was there.

It was a repeat of the additional burden I carried about how much people would think about my decision to leave Disney (they weren't thinking about me), how I might be judged as a first-time author relative to the success of my then wife (there were no real comparisons), or the worry of how close I might feel connected to my adopted daughter relative to my bio kids (I've never one time looked at her and thought, "Oh, there's my adopted daughter"; she's just my daughter). It's just part of our human nature to imagine all the scenarios and then fixate on the worry of how we'll process the worst, were those cases to emerge.

They very rarely do.

The things that do actually happen are a microscopic subset of the things that can happen, which is a tiny subset of all the things we worry about. It's bananas.

Worrying about what might happen is *totally wasted emotion.*

When I woke up the following morning for the first time in an empty house, I pulled out a journal and wrote down these words: "Last night was hard, but it didn't win." The night came nowhere near the story I'd manufactured. That's the thing about our fear: it's only when we walk through our anxiety that we are able to see how divergent our stories and our realities have been. Only then are we able to disengage ourselves from them.

That next morning I threw my running shoes on and got back on the road, back on a rock in nature when I was done, talking to a higher power who was still there. As I sat there, I experienced an overwhelming feeling of hope and strength born out of seeing that this thing I dreaded was a thing I could handle. But more important, I was able to see how the weight I'd afforded the night in the lead-up made the experience worse than it needed to be; seeing it helped me to consciously work to avoid making the same mistake in the windows that would precede our first holiday in a new normal, transitioning away from my company, diving into the dating pool after a twenty-year hiatus, and a myriad of other new things along the way.

It doesn't necessarily mean it will be easy. It doesn't imply the headwinds won't make you cry. Trust me, I'm awesome, and there have been times in my evolution where I was the Cal Ripken Jr. of crying over consecutive days. It simply means it won't be as bad as you think.

The words of Marcus Aurelius are as relevant today as they were two thousand years ago: "You have power over your mind, not outside events. Realize this, and you will find strength." Hold this truth in the journey ahead. You cannot control what will happen next, and worrying about it will not affect a thing other than distracting you from the task at hand, wasting your mental energy, compromising your courage, undermining your motivation, and slowing your pace.

You cannot control what happens next, which means you can stop worrying about it. Be free.

LOGBOOK

JOURNALING ACTIVITY

One of the best ways to let go of the worry of what might happen is to create an empowering belief around why you'll be ready even if something goes sideways. Grab your journal and go through the following exercise on the first blank page:

- Write out one thing that you're currently afraid of in the "unknowns ahead" bucket. (Example: I might fail publicly trying something new.)
- Identify three limiting beliefs you're holding onto that keep you from believing you'll be able to handle this situation if it were to unfold. (Example: I'm not strong enough to deal with failing; people will judge me for not being great immediately; I'll be exposed as unqualified.)
- Now create three columns on your paper: Positive Outcomes, Negative Outcomes, and Reframed Outcomes. Make a list of everything that could happen, both negative and positive, were this imagined scenario to come true. Once you have a full list, reframe the negatives into another way to see them. (Example: if you were to lose your job, a positive outcome is that you might find a better one; a negative outcome is that you'd need money to live; and a reframe of the negative is that providing for your family may force you to explore different industries, grow your network, and consider a side hustle as a bridge.)

- Now go back to your three limiting beliefs and restate them as empowering beliefs. (Example: I've already made it through 100 percent of my hard days so I know I can do hard things. The only way I've ever grown was by getting better over time. Failure is the price of entry for the life I'm already qualified for.)

WHAT CAN HAPPEN

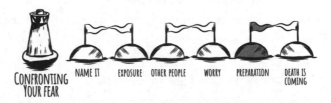

I recently got a text from my next-door neighbor. A warning of sorts. It turned out that he saw a snake slithering on the path that separates his property from mine. He warned that he believed it to be venomous and that it was last seen heading into my yard. With the four kids and mini schnauzer that live on this property in the middle of nowhere Texas, he wanted to make sure we were keeping an eye out for imminent danger.

But what it made me aware of, in a way that I had not been as aware as I should have been as a person who lives in the wilderness on a piece of land that literally shares a boundary with a bison ranch, is that, of course, snakes have *always* been present on my land. The fact that I got visual confirmation of a snake in my yard immediately and forever changed the way that I was conscious of the always-present danger of snakes as a thing that I needed to be on the lookout for as we wandered in the high grass of our adventures out back.

I had been aware that theoretically snakes were a danger, but I didn't put on tall shoes or keep my kids from running after a ball that flew into the brush. But now that I had the confirmation of their existence, it changed the way I took seriously the very real dangers that exist in the middle of nowhere, where the grass grows tall.

The text happened to come about a month into the global pandemic. For me, it came to represent the idea that the knowledge of what *could* happen can be a catalyst for preparing ourselves just in case that thing *does* happen. In the last chapter, I encouraged you not to worry about what *might* happen. However, releasing yourself from the worry of *might* doesn't absolve you of preparing for the things that *can*. As we've discussed, this journey requires preparation and a responsibility to acknowledge the things that can happen so that you're ready in case they do.

If 2020 taught us anything, it was the importance of being ready to roll with the punches. As much as no one could have been fully prepared for the impact of a global pandemic, some people had emergency savings. Intellectually, everyone understands why this is a good idea. But practically, only those who built it into their financial plan were afforded a little more sleep at night when unemployment and job insecurity reached lifetime highs. The habits and routines that we create in good times? They aren't there necessarily to keep us going in the good. They're there to allow us the ability to weather the storms in the bad.

Reaching for the audacity of your vision requires that you inventory the things that can happen along the journey and create contingency plans to accommodate the possibility that things don't go as you expect. When you're pushing into new terrain, things rarely go as you expect.

A good sailor goes through their pre-departure checklist, but that list also includes those things to include in the *what if things go wrong* catalog of supplies like the GPS tracker, the contact onshore, the extra water and food, and a change of clothes. Doing so creates a level of confidence and reinforces their courage in a way that allows them to head out to sea knowing that, irrespective of the conditions, they're ready.

The antidote to fear is a plan.

Understanding the things that can come up along this journey and preemptively considering how you'll handle whatever presents itself is how you cultivate courage.

What if you get moving on these dreams and run into financial trouble? What kind of emergency fund have you established to weather a short-term storm? How are you making decisions that don't compromise your ability to maintain your responsibilities to your family?

What if you leave the familiar for the unknown and find yourself triggered by insecurity or impostor syndrome? What kind of habits and routines do you need to commit to now so that when these feelings inevitably show up (and they will), you will know how to process them with positive coping mechanisms?

How will you handle failure along the way? What kind of community are you surrounding yourself with to share the experience of your loss in a way that helps you dust yourself off and get back up? What kinds of tools and resources will you invest in to help you normalize the inevitable feelings that you'll process when you don't get it perfectly right the first time?

Part of the exercise of writing the letter from your fear is the hope that you can create visual confirmation of the things that can happen, so that in seeing them as you set off on your journey, you're able to construct the contingencies for how you'll handle them before you find yourself stuck inside of them.

The gift of this text from a neighbor, like the gift of a pandemic that nobody asked for, was the wake-up call to prepare for the things that have always existed and can always happen. Once you know, it's something you can't unknow, so use the gift that's been afforded to consider how you'll handle the things that can come up in a way that builds the confidence and courage that acts as an antidote to the fear of them possibly presenting themselves.

We still play in the yard. We just wear tall boots when we do. Pulling those boots on gives us the permission to enjoy the experience in a way that doesn't disregard what could happen, but keeps us safe just in case it does. Whatever your version of tall boots is, pull them on, get brave as you face your fear, and enjoy the ride.

LOGBOOK

JOURNALING ACTIVITY

Did you save that letter from your fear? Pull it out, and put the fear items you listed into three buckets: Financial, Health, and Relationships. These are the primary sources of our anxieties; they are places where preemptively developing a contingency plan can prepare us for whatever conditions are thrown our way. What will you do if money gets tough? If someone gets sick? If a relationship sours or needs emergency attention? The hope is that you can start building a contingency plan for each of these three buckets so that you can plan now to be prepared for "if and when."

WHAT WILL HAPPEN

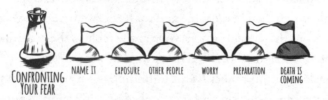

CONFRONTING YOUR FEAR — NAME IT — EXPOSURE — OTHER PEOPLE — WORRY — PREPARATION — DEATH IS COMING

In 2005, Steve Jobs gave one of the greatest commencement speeches of all time at Stanford University.

> When I was seventeen, I read a quote that went something like: "If you live each day as if it was your last, someday you'll most certainly be right."

He goes on to suggest that when he confronts his mortality, it affords him an ability to ask if what he's going to do in the day ahead is something that fuels him. Change comes when the answer isn't "yes." Like Jobs, we only have a limited time on this earth. When we can stay connected to this reality, we're free from thinking we have something to lose by going after our dreams. As Jobs said in that commencement speech, "There is no reason not to follow your heart."

Death is a guarantee. It absolutely will happen for every one of us, and it is just about the only thing we can be sure of in life. What's crazy is that many of us spend most of our lives afraid of dying, when the promise of death should be the thing that gives us life. This knowledge should be the greatest catalyst ever for doing everything we can with the limited time we have.

Fear can be a great motivator. In fact it's the motivation I tap into most when I think about who I want to become. There are people who are driven by the visualization of all they can be someday. But I tap into a darker, more powerful force. What might it feel like to miss the opportunity to fully live into who I was meant to be? I lean into something called the power of negative visualization.

In the depths of a glorious midlife crisis around age forty, desperate for the answers to the bigger existential questions of why I was here and where my fulfillment might be found, I imagined my sixtieth birthday dinner. Seated at the table were my now-adult children, my closest friends, anyone and everyone who mattered most in my life. On big birthdays in my family, we always go around the table and toast the honoree, recognizing the contributions they'd made to everyone at the table in the years that led to this monumental threshold, and this would be my toast.

My vision for this dinner had it unfolding in one of two ways. In the first, the people around the table get choked up with emotion during their speeches, in tears for the impact I've had on their lives. My tears meeting theirs, I get up from the table and share a long hug with each guest before the next person dives in on their gushing report on a life well lived. The room is so full that it's standing room only, and this celebration goes on for hours. I can see it like a movie playing in my head.

In the other version, some of my grown children don't show. Those that do don't have much to say. There's no need for standing room as the table sits with empty seats and the tears that flow aren't those of joy, but regret. Sadness for what could have been. Disgust for how the last twenty years could have gone. Wasted. There's shame instead of pride. Pity replacing embraces.

This movie plays in my head too. This is the visual that keeps me asking what it will take to show up for my life and those who I love. This negative visualization causes me to put my running shoes on when I don't feel like it, has me choosing a therapy session over a drink. These are the images that I most fear, and I leverage that fear to motivate me to do it anyway on the days I don't feel like it.

A couple years back, we were hit with unexpected news of the passing of my brother-in-law. Gone way before his time, snatched in an instant. Devastating news that sent shock waves through our family. As we gathered to celebrate his life, the funeral ended with a touching tribute of pictures in a slideshow to some of his favorite music. Not a dry eye in the house. Each of us remembering something great about someone great, gone too soon.

As I sat there remembering Michael, I couldn't help but consider the slideshow at my own service one day. The reality hit me that I was the sole owner of every image in the slideshow of every day that was left in my life. The way I honored the intention of my creator, met the needs of my family, led with a servant's heart to those I'm in community with. That I, as the author of this life, had a say in how spectacular that memorial would be with the way I filled every day I have left with the memorable experiences, love for family, the acts of service, the work of impact that would ultimately create the way I would be remembered once I was gone. How I might honor my maker with my work here on earth.

I've been given enormous gifts by our creator. All of us have. Over our kitchen table hangs a sign with a family mission statement of sorts. Among the words written on it: *to whom much is given, much is expected.* I know that I can't fight time. I know that one day I will die. I know that when I get to the end, be it sixty or one hundred, I want to have a celebration of a life well lived. A life that honored the gifts I was given. A life that makes me as proud as those who might raise a glass at my birthday or eulogize me at my funeral.

What kind of toast do you envision for your milestone birthday twenty years from now?

What kind of video will they play at your funeral to commemorate the way you took what was given and made the absolute most of it?

The call to journey out on these choppy seas isn't an invitation so much as a mandate. It's the call to each of us to fully exploit our gifts, in order that those gifts might serve others in our lives who so desperately need them.

As Tim Ferriss once said, "The hard choices, what we most fear doing, asking, saying, these are very often what we most need to do." Heeding the call of this mandate to fully unleash the gifts that exist inside of you may scare you unlike anything you've ever known before. Which is why you know you have to take the step off the dock and onto the boat. The seas are calling. Some of you will fear the choppy water; some may even fear death. I fear not fully living while I'm alive.

Jobs ended his speech with these words:

Your time is limited, so don't waste it living someone else's life. Don't be trapped by dogma—which is living with the results of other people's think-ing. Don't let the noise of others' opinions drown out your own inner voice. And most important, have the courage to follow your heart and intuition. They somehow already know what you truly want to become. Everything else is secondary.

Or, in the words of Andy Dufresne inside the walls of the Shawshank Prison, "Get busy living, or get busy dying." Living it is.

LOGBOOK

JOURNALING ACTIVITY

Cast the two visions of your birthday twenty years from now, best case and worst case. What are people toasting to in the good? Why are people disappointed in the bad? Which of these visions motivates you the most? Prepare yourself to use the motivation that comes from both to create the plan to engineer the best possible scenario.

WHAT IT'S GOING TO TAKE

In 2019, I met with every business leader I could to understand how to scale the company we were building. People in direct-to-consumer businesses, personality-driven businesses, media companies, and those working in the personal development space that we were growing inside of. As much as there was wisdom that came from each of these opportunities to learn from people who were further along their journey than we were, who'd made mistakes and were willing to share what they learned from them, there was a single piece of advice that came up over and over again: you need to pass the "bus test." As in, how do we diversify the business in a way that allows the tools we're affording to exist if our primary revenue source (Rachel) weren't here, if she was unable to work for some length of time, or (one day a long time from now) is gone?

YOU GOTTA HAVE FAITH

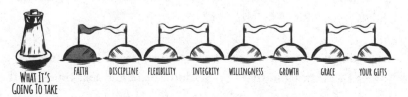

At the time, I was feeling a call to step into something that terrified me. To move from operating in a business to leaning into the gifts I'd been given to be a voice of the business. To move from someone in a behind-the-scenes role to someone who might step into using his words as a first-time author, podcast host, and online coach in 2020. Such a move would not only offset the enormous weight that was being carried by my then wife, but it would also unlock the purpose of my life. Writing a book would require radical transparency and confidence that I had the skills to helm a solo show or lead people through transformation in their lives or careers via coaching. While I'd heard the call, I also heard those same voices that you might, second-guessing my qualifications to step fully into the role.

At this same time, I got a direct message on Instagram from someone I didn't know named Jared. He and his wife had attended a business conference we'd thrown. As they left, he said he felt a call to send me a note a day. A good word. Often a prayer. He could have never appreciated how much I'd need the reassurance.

Jared, Nov. 14, 2019: Praying today for strength and endurance. Be strong and courageous today.

It was six weeks ahead of my pushing out into a new year filled with scary unknowns. It was the word I needed that day when I didn't even know it. As the turn of the year gave way to stepping out of the operation of the business, into the launch of my first-time coaching, Jared sent a note every single day. Encouragement that unbelievably felt ordained. It was just what I needed. The day before my first live coaching sessions to the moderately overwhelming five thousand students who'd signed up, he hit me with what would help me courageously step into this new endeavor.

Jared, Jan. 13, 2020: May you sense clarity and confidence over the week ahead.

And I did. Yes, it was imperfect and I was nervous and there were plenty of things I was taking in that I could do to be better next time, but the community of coaching students poured as much back to me as I attempted to pour into them. Affirming there was good in this work. A worthwhile endeavor in this pivot into something that brought me from behind the scenes to something more forward facing. Not only helping offset my partner's carrying weight, but more important, connecting me for the first time in forever to the unlocking of the gifts that sat inside.

That lasted for four minutes.

The upcoming launch of my first book had me questioning if it was a good idea. The decision to write it had sparked my insecurity. What if I were revealed to be unworthy as an author? What if I were found out as a person who didn't deserve the opportunity to write a page, let alone a book? As the book launched into the world, once again there was a word from Jared, saying what I needed to hear on a day I needed to hear it.

> Jared, March 12, 2020: I encourage you to be a light in your area of influence. People are seeking out hope. I have been praying that you wouldn't process the fears of today like the world.

At the time, I thought I was sent Jared to encourage me as I stepped into this new attempt to use my words and voice to teach. It wasn't until my divorce that I had the perspective to appreciate that Jared was also sent to plant seeds of perpetual faithfulness so that I could lean on it when I needed it most. The day we announced our divorce, he sent me this message:

> Jared, June 9, 2020: Dave, may you receive this message with love and care. Upon reading your marriage update, I immediately heard God above my own thoughts. It's even clearer now than it was seven months ago. I am to continue to be a source of hope and encouragement to you. More important than that, I hope you see in this message that God sees you and loves you. Praying today for protection, discernment, and for time and space to process. Love ya brother.

Tears. I simply responded with gratitude for the gift that he had been. Acknowledged that I had been connected to my faith more in the past seven months than I had in a long time. That the proximity to this higher power was afforded in so many respects because of the generosity of a stranger heeding a call to show up.

In that first week of the announcement, Jared was joined by a cast of friends and family who would also generously offer their support in a hard time. Among the most impactful was Jason Morriss, the pastor of my home church, Austin New Church. In what felt uncanny at the time, similar to Jared, I began receiving a message a day, in this case the same message every day from Jason for the first two months of my divorce. The simplest and most powerful eleven words imaginable:

What small piece of sadness can I hold for you today?

Every single day, this offer to alleviate a small piece of this burden of grief was a signal of solidarity from a higher power promising not to let me walk through the pain alone.

Two weeks later, about a mile into my daily run to process my feelings and thoughts, I was stopped by a golf cart on the long country road that leads to my house. In the cart sat four strangers, two grown and two small, who greeted my head-down headphones-wearing self with an enthusiastic set of smiles that felt a bit like that person who sits down next to you on a plane and is ready to become your new best friend. I wasn't feeling it, wasn't interested. If this was the phone call letting me know "I might already be a winner," the inn here was full.

But for whatever reason that day, though I was deep in a valley of grief and confusion about what *next* looked like, after I gave the cursory nod-and-wave combo, I stopped and turned around. I introduced myself to find that these were my new neighbors. To the terror of other Texans, another group of Californians had migrated to this beautiful, spacious oasis.

It was the beginning of the bromance of the millennium, the introduction of Brady as my new best friend, his wife, Lynn, and their two kids as part of my new, weird single-dad family. We barbecued on the daily. His two kids the ages of my youngest are together, thick as thieves. We recruited a neighbor to help dig out a dirt track in the backyard for go-karts. Added a few lounge chairs, and voilà! One part neighbors, one

part therapists, one part cheerleading squad, and always available friends. Sent in when I needed them most.

The therapist who helped me discover who I was, now that I was no longer who I'd been? Sent in this time.

The gaggle of other friends who'd populate the backyard's newly furnished patio set? Sent in this time with regularity.

The extraordinary woman going through her own divorce who agreed to sit for a podcast that we never got to because of my tears? A woman who became not just an empathetic ear but a beacon of hope? Sent in this time.

The neighbors who offered us unlimited access to a pond where we were reminded that, even in hard times, the fish still bite? A blessing sent in this time.

The new habits, the fight for peace, the closeness with my kids, a found love of reading? All sent in this time.

On this journey, you must have faith that the people, resources, and belief in self that you'll need to reach your destination will show up in this time. They will come in the form of small miracles every single day. Micro-blessings. What I can say definitively is that the emergence of each of these signals of faith acted as an invitation to draw closer to the sender. The more I stepped in faith, toward faith, the more I was able to see faithfulness.

As I'm writing this today, this is the note that Jared sent this morning:

Jared, January 15, 2021: May we be light in the darkness today. May we be part of the solution. I believe we will see goodness.

Of course he sent that today. Amen.

Now I don't know if you have religious beliefs or not, but the takeaway from this chapter isn't so much about that kind of faith as much as the idea that you have to have faith, belief that the things you don't even know you'll need will present themselves to support you and your journey along the way. At its simplest, faith is complete trust and confidence in something. It often exists in the absence of evidence. That said, I've found when you lean into faith with 100 percent certainty, the evidence presents itself along the way.

It may be a relationship to a higher power, your connection to the universe working on behalf of your greater good, a belief that good energy attracts good energy, the promise of nature or justice or a Jedi prevailing over the Dark Side. I used to think you had to choose one, but now I believe that all of these forces come together for my good. The act of regular prayer, intentional meditation, creating space for mindfulness, community aligned with my values, everyday optimism, they all come together to support my journey. They do so because of my belief that they will.

During my time at The Hollis Company, Rachel developed a line of successful daily gratitude and intentional goal-setting journals in our Start Today brand. Every day you ground yourself in gratitude by listing five great things from the previous day followed by a list of ten things that you're working toward as goals. In the vision-casting for the goals, the prompts were dreams that had not yet happened, but that were written in the present tense as if they already had. Among mine from this morning:

I am an Iron Man finisher.

I have published a Tea Time children's book.

I have an exceptional co-parenting relationship that creates a stable, consistent environment for my kids.

Stating goals this way is a consciousness hack. It makes the mind believe these dreams exist in real time. Your mind then scans the landscape every day for ways to align the belief in those dreams with the things that would also have to be true to make them exist. Think of it as connecting dots in the required work, the necessary relationships, and the fuel for the brainstorm of what to do next time you're stuck. Speaking these goals in present tense is an act of faith. Believing that they will come to be even when there's no evidence to support the belief.

In the journey that lies ahead, courage is cultivated as much in the belief that you will reach your destination as in the faith that the things required to get you there will show up when you need them. As you push away from the safe harbor, you must have faith to see that the evidence will present itself along the way.

LOGBOOK

JOURNALING ACTIVITY

Make a list of your ten dreams and write them out in present tense. Write them every single day as though they've already happened, in a posture of faith that they will. As you do, tune your focus for the evidence that will present itself to support you on your journey and stay on the hunt for the dots that connect to make the belief that they're already true come to be.

KEEPING THE WATER OUT

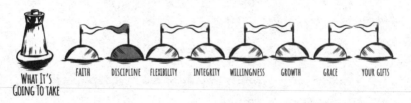

There's an old proverb that's critical for the journey into the unknowns at sea:

> Ships don't sink because of the water around them. Ships sink because of the water that gets in them. Don't let what's happening around you get inside you and weigh you down.

It's why we've talked about releasing ourselves from the worry of what other people think, the importance of connecting to our "why," the mandate to fortify ourselves with the right approach to all aspects of health, the ways we use perspective and mindset and everything else to defend against the water we might take on.

But as we embark on this pursuit of unlocking our purpose, it also comes with a responsibility as captain of this mission to anticipate the two essential ways that our success could be undermined, even sunk, before we arrive at our destination:

- The boundaries necessary to keep *other people* from saturating our ship with their form of toxic water (fear, negativity, judgment, competing values . . .) in a way that impedes or altogether upends our progress.
- The radical honesty necessary to create the self-awareness for how we might let our own fear and insecurity bring water onboard in a way that sabotages the chances of reaching our dreamed-of port before we get there.

Setting boundaries with others, especially those we love or crave love from, is one of the hardest and most important things we can ever do. Boundaries are a form of self-care. They exist as a reflection of the respect we believe ourselves to be worthy of. They are a requirement for maintaining sanity as a cornerstone of good mental health. Boundaries protect and preserve your courage and they must exist to maintain momentum in this pursuit of the life you're moving toward.

For lifelong people pleasers, boundaries can be extremely difficult to set. The hard part about a boundary is that your decision to say "yes" to something that moves you closer to your intended outcome may be at the expense of someone else's expectations, personal agenda, and comfort. Every time your calendar reflects your values, your calling, your growth, your priorities, it often won't align perfectly with people you've afforded weight to and historically accommodated in your life.

The real test shows up when the people who've given you some of what you've needed (their attention, affection, "liking" you) change their tune when you draw boundaries. Your mind will even play tricks on you, convincing you that somehow you're "wrong" because of this reaction that comes as a result of their newfound discomfort. Is it possible that standing in your truth shows more of who *they* really are? Might you have peace in appreciating that when you started acting "right" it revealed their true colors? That your decision to truly be you revealed a side of them that doesn't support who you really are and who you're becoming?

You'll have to make a choice: either keep *them* happy at the expense of you becoming your greatest self and honoring your truth, or believe that living into your calling and becoming who you were meant to be is an acceptable trade-off for frustrating the people who'd prefer you stay where you are. Not giving in to those who feel safer when you play it safe. Respectfully pushing aside the worry of those accustomed to who you've been, not allowing their fear that you might outgrow them bias your belief in your ability. Working intentionally every day to avoid second-guessing your intuition and eroding your courage by allowing someone who isn't ready to challenge their own status quo or feels threatened by your belief that you were called to something greater.

One of my longest-standing friendships happens to be with someone who's an eternal pessimist. He's a "grass is always browner" kind of guy. Rather than seeing everything that could go right, he'll itemize and inventory everything that's likely to go wrong. When the market moves down on three consecutive days, he's certain we're heading for recession. When he got a recent promotion, we spent more time talking about the taxes he'd pay than we did about how he could finally afford a vacation with his kids. I love this man like a brother, and also, he's not invited to the table when I start dreaming about where I'm heading. His perspective, mindset, and hopefulness, or lack thereof, invite the water I'm trying to keep out in a way that threatens my ability to stay afloat.

The same goes for anyone trying to disguise their judgment as advice or their fear as "I'm just looking out for you." While I can appreciate that these people may be operating out of what they truly believe are their best intentions (and mine), they won't have to live with the regret of not fully exploiting my gifts at the end of my life. They will not die with my unrealized dreams. They will not wonder how much more light I might have offered to the world if only I'd better guarded my mind from the distractive forces that had me second-guessing myself. But I will.

So, in the pursuit of actualizing who I was created to be, the boundaries that exist to hold *them* at arm's length are what actually give me a fighting chance to allow me to become me. All of me. Fully me. The very best version of who I was placed on this planet to be.

Those same boundaries exist in the way I intentionally and regularly audit the trailing twelve months of my calendar, whom I follow on social media, the way I moderate the amount of news I watch, and how I consider any content I consume regularly. If the way I've spent my time does not support the way I need to spend my time going forward, new boundaries must be set. If the influences that I'm immersed in every day negatively affect my thinking or compromise my belief in self, they must go. It's not a nice-to-have, but a nonnegotiable for maintaining the trajectory of who I'm becoming.

The second, and arguably even more important consideration in how we might allow this water into our ship, into our life, is the willingness to look within. Understanding the unhealthy coping mechanisms, bad habits, and negative self-talk that sink our chances. The sabotage we create that can only be avoided if we're willing to own our weaknesses honestly. It's the difficult work of bringing our shame into the light, addressing it in a way that unshackles the drag that it creates. Acknowledging our insecurities honestly to build the routine, guardrails, community, and plans necessary to prevent our weaknesses from undermining everything we're working toward.

For example, in my last book, I talked about the way that alcohol had been a coping mechanism that I leaned on to relieve stress, mute discomfort, and avoid dealing with the insecurities that come up when we push into the uncertainty that produces growth. This vice that had been a casual part of my life tipped to an unhealthy way of avoiding all the feelings of identity change in leaving Disney, the challenges of entrepreneurship, and the friction in partnering with my spouse in our business endeavors. Though I longed for fulfillment, I was eliminating the opportunity to achieve it by blotting out the lessons I could learn were I actually to sit in those uncomfortable feelings.

Negative coping mechanisms are not a local anesthetic.

You can't mute the stress without muting the joy. You can't eliminate your insecurities without eliminating your opportunity for growth. I was trying to smooth the rough edges that came in the discomfort of growth, when the rough edges are actually the only way to grow. Whether it's booze or food or sex or overworking or anything else, it's one or the other. You either get a handle on how you cope or you miss out on growth and stay stuck. You either keep the water out of your boat or you sink. You can't have both.

So, at the time of writing my last book, I decided to eliminate alcohol altogether for a year. Made the decision to show myself I could, but more than anything did so in the attempt to fully receive the benefits of the growth that I was so interested in pursuing in the first place. And here's what I learned:

- I can do anything. Making and keeping this promise about a thing that has casually been part of my life for twenty-five years means I can make and keep a promise about literally anything that's always been part of my life.
- I had to find a substitute. I traded drinking for running. When I felt triggered, I got out on the road to digest what I was feeling in a way that actually allowed me to process and grow rather than suppress and stagnate.
- Better coping doesn't reduce the triggers. My ability to productively work through stress actually allowed a greater capacity for thriving outside my comfort zone and reframing failure. So, I just had to run. A lot. Healthily processing along the way.
- Not drinking was great for my health. Yes, I lost nineteen pounds, but beyond the physical, I'm talking about my mental health, spiritual health, sexual health. All the healths.
- Owning my struggle gave me power. I took a thing that brought me shame and turned it into one of my proudest accomplishments. I did it by talking honestly to everyone in my life about my choice and the "why" behind it. Your power can come in owning your struggle.
- I got to normalize struggle and habits with my kids. They were along for the ride, including the dinner celebration when I hit the goal at the end.

I wish that my story of giving up drinking ended here, with me healthy and running every day instead of turning to alcohol. But then my divorce happened. I was dealing with an incredible amount of grief and pain over our ending. And I drank to cope. Two sad days of numbing the pain with alcohol in a dark room alone. Which only made me feel worse. This was not who I wanted to be.

On the third day, I had one of those tough talks with myself in the mirror. Who did I want to be? How did I want to process hard things? Did I want to make them harder or did I want to grow? I chose growth, and on day three, I stopped drinking and started running. Again.

I also turned to my faith, every day, all day. And I leaned on therapy, writing, focusing on my kids, friends, and my health, including sobriety. Again.

During one of those runs immediately following our breakup, I heard a sermon from Pastor Steven Furtick about storms. His big takeaway: It's not the first storm that necessarily gets people . . . it's the secondary storm that people *create* in reaction to that storm that takes them down. The way we *react* to the storm we didn't expect leading to our demise. In this journey ahead, there will be storms. It is a guarantee. You will not choose the day your world gets interrupted, you will not enjoy it, but your decision about how you handle it determines how you weather it.

There's a parable in the Bible about two houses, one built on sand, the other on rock. When these houses face the same storm, the first is destroyed while the other stands strong. Your foundation determines your outcome. Being honest about and owning your coping mechanisms can be the difference between taking on water and staying afloat.

I think all of us have a thing we carry shame for. Probably a few things. The demons that, if left unchecked, will sabotage our chances. Sink our ship. So often our unwillingness to acknowledge our weakness is born out of pride and cemented in shame. The worry of what asking for help might say about us acting as the barrier to getting it. The pride of wanting to keep up appearances allowing that shame to fester and grow in the dark.

Your weakness is a reflection of your humanity, not an indictment. It doesn't mean you aren't good or worthy or enough. Your willingness to own your weakness and bring it into the light is one of the greatest showcases of strength. That kind of strength is a prerequisite for unlocking your purpose and the full pursuit of your gifts.

So, in yet another book, I'll own my weaknesses and the work I'm doing (and will have to do imperfectly and to the best of my ability for the rest of my life) to keep it from capsizing my ship. I want to share my struggle in part to normalize it as a fellow human, but also in the hope that it gives you permission to own yours. It's going to take radical honesty, an abundance of grace, a community that supports you through accountability, and a willingness to do the one thing that can inoculate you from the shame, pride, and self-loathing that might keep you from addressing it: *own it by bringing it into the light.*

Ships sink because of the water that gets into them. Be it water that we allow others to pour in, or the water we pour in ourselves, the onus is on us to keep that water out. The only way we'll stay afloat for the voyage ahead is if we're willing to do the work of establishing boundaries from the forces that can compromise our courage by talking us out of trusting our intuition. And it takes the even harder work of being frank about how we get in our own way. It's only when we address both, honestly and proactively, that we give ourselves the chance to stay afloat.

LOGBOOK

JOURNALING ACTIVITY

What is your thing? The go-to unhealthy coping mechanism that will let water into the boat? What's the secondary storm that you'll create in reaction to the storm that will unexpectedly hit? Binge eating? Workaholism? Sex? Booze? Negative self-talk? Aggression? Prescription pills? Shame will not serve you in the mission ahead. Pride for not wanting to ask for help guarantees you won't get it. Keeping your negative coping mechanism in the dark promises that it will fester and grow until it steals your courage when things get hard. Bring it into the light, share it with the people you love most, and make a plan to preempt reaching for it when you're triggered.

FLEXIBILITY REQUIRED AHEAD

A little more than twenty years ago, I worked at the grassroots marketing arm of a company called Merv Griffin Productions. My job was to take our clients' products and put them in front of prospective customers in unconventional places. I developed college campus tours for a variety of big magazines, a satellite extension of a short-lived gameshow on Fox, a spring break street team for MTV, and a host of other zany things that played to my personality and twenty-five-year-old stamina as a road warrior.

Though most of the projects I managed were for things that either no longer exist or that nobody cares about, being assigned the Columbia Records account introduced the single exception to that rule. With a mandate to help launch their new recording artists, I became the tour manager for a relatively unknown trio from Houston called Destiny's Child.

Now I appreciate that this may sound fancy, but that's because you likely know who Beyoncé, Kelly Rowland, and Michelle Williams are. You may even shimmy a little when "Say My Name" or "Bills, Bills, Bills" comes on from the breakout album we were crossing the country to launch. But at the time, trust me, this was far from whatever you're thinking. I know this because the tour I was running didn't go through the stadium circuit they could fill today.

We were playing the center court of the local shopping mall. Drawing crowds of a little more than a hundred people.

As tour manager and head of craft services, I was responsible for overseeing the building of the stage and for fetching lunch. Hot-Dog-On-A-Stick may have been involved.

The bottom line is, we were working on a smaller budget with the hope that this tour would coincide with radio support, a single release, critical response, and getting lucky. The events hoped to play a small part of this big machine that in success would take their music and notoriety to

another level. We could never have predicted the trajectory of this band over the time frame of this tour.

When we got to the first venue, after the ladies were resting in the "greenroom" (which was a conference room down the hallway from a Foot Locker), I made sure the stage was being assembled, the sound system worked, the vinyl tablecloths with Beyoncé's, Kelly's, and Michelle's faces on the front that I made at Kinko's were placed straight. Once the crowd gathered, I'd pass out the wristbands, introduce an opening singer from a local high school, and then count the crowd down. Each show started the same way, with Beyoncé singing the national anthem (felt right) before a four-song set. Once they were done singing, before returning to the tour bus, they'd sign autographs on the posters I'd packed from the previous city.

We'd wake up the next day and do it all over again. It was just as fancy as it sounds.

Except it wasn't the same thing over and over each day. Each day, the electricity in the air and crowd size grew.

In most cases, this is what you're hoping for. As a tour manager who'd long ago confirmed the amount of security and the number of wristbands, speakers, and posters necessary, what began with a couple hundred people in the first week of the tour gave way to a couple thousand by the third.

And as much as we were firsthand witnesses to a group becoming who they were always meant to be, this chapter isn't about finally getting there, but rather the kind of on-the-fly flexibility required to get there when your plans start taking off. Every single plan I'd built for how this tour would go was completely upended by the unpredictably steep trajectory of their emergence on the national scene. When your plans anticipate a commercial flight and you end up on a rocket ship, you need new plans.

The plans I made at the beginning of that nationwide tour with Destiny's Child were not the plans that would have allowed us to finish the tour successfully. The tools I'd used for a couple hundred people at the start were wildly inadequate to handle the demands of the many thousands that were attending by the end. An entirely new approach was a mandate to deliver quality, assure safety, keep talent happy, and leave guests walking away with a "brand deposit" kind of experience.

I recently sat with my friend, the inspirational powerhouse and former monk Jay Shetty. His *New York Times* bestselling book, *Think Like a Monk,* provided so many helpful tips on how to get to where we want to go by challenging the ways we've always thought and questioning the tools we've historically used. In our conversation, he brought up a story told by the Buddha.

A man goes on a journey and comes upon a fast-flowing river. He needs to get to the other side to continue his way and notices bamboo sticks and a rope that might afford a chance to make a raft. So, he lays out the bamboo and ties them tight and fashions a small craft that will give him a chance to make it across this swift body of water.

To his astonishment, it works. It works well. As he steps off to the new shore, there is an appreciation, a reverence even for the way this raft kept his journey going. How this raft, in the most treacherous part of the crossing, literally saved his life. If not for that raft, he wouldn't have come this far, and in that moment, the decision is made to never again move forward without that raft by his side.

Raft strapped to his back, the journey continues. The adventure turns into a new stage and in this next level, introduces a densely wooded forest. Trees are mere inches apart and the man finds himself trying to maneuver and squeeze his way through, believing there has to be a way to keep this tool that's been so valuable to his journey thus far intact, even as he keeps hitting resistance in this new terrain.

It's there that the lesson of what it will take to continue on the journey is learned. An epiphany that the only way forward is to let go of what got him there. The revelation that the thing that saved his life was now the thing that would prevent him from having one if he continued to cling to it.

The plans that work in the harbor don't work at sea. The game inside of comfort is drastically different from the one you play chasing growth. New game, new playbook. As we think about what it will take to pursue your calling, one of the most important things you'll have to do is make peace with the reality that you will not be able to rely on the things that worked in the past, even those things that previously transformed your life. If you want to play at the next level, you'll need next-level habits and routines, a next-level circle of friends and mentors, a next-level approach to all aspects of your health, and a next-level mindset fueled by an evolved sense of and belief in self. As a wise, unknown person once said, "Until you change your thinking, you will always recycle your experiences."

Near the end of the Destiny's Child tour, they introduced a song off their next album, the album that would change everything for each of them forever. The album was called *Survivor* and the title track is, to this day, a theme song for anyone going through anything.

Your calling is here. Stepping into it will reveal just how strong you really are. The challenges of new terrain that are inevitable as you step into your true self will build a resilience, a confidence, a grit that you would have never known if not for what you'll have to push through. Everything that you'll become is forged in surviving the choppy, chaotic water along the way. And as it turns out, survival, when the waters start moving fast, may just come down to letting go of what you've known to learn something new. To release how you've always done it, so that you can start doing it the way it's going to need to be done when you get to where you're going.

Keep going. Let go. Stay flexible to keep on surviving.

LOGBOOK

JOURNALING ACTIVITY

Consider how you've managed change over your life. Pivoting your approach and processing change is inevitable in the decision to leave the harbor. Having the courage to embrace the inevitability is a necessity for what's ahead. Make a list of five things that you've handled well when it comes to change, and five things that have been challenging or triggering when things don't go as expected.

IF/THEN

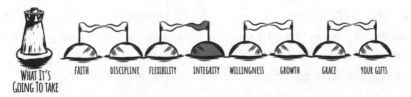

WHAT IT'S GOING TO TAKE · FAITH · DISCIPLINE · FLEXIBILITY · INTEGRITY · WILLINGNESS · GROWTH · GRACE · YOUR GIFTS

My approach to engineering my best year ever was backward. As I sat on that rock outside Tucson, my attempt to build the most exceptional future possible had me searching for where I'd been at my worst in my past. Looking back over the previous five years to find the times when I couldn't connect to my courage, struggled to feel proud, felt stuck, wrestled with shame, had my confidence compromised and my motivation impaired. The attempt to measure good times versus bad led to a powerful question:

How do I feel about myself when I'm by myself?

My thought process was that if I could identify all the times when I didn't feel the way I'd hope to when I was by myself, then maybe there would be a theme. If I could know which variables were present in each of those low moments, it might give me the opportunity to build a plan to eliminate those variables when they come up or preempt them from happening in the first place.

To my surprise, there was a single, glaring, consistent variable present in every memory of being stuck. Every time I didn't feel good about myself when I was by myself, it was because of incongruence. Dissonance that existed between who I hoped to be and how I was showing up in my life. The space between who I could have been and who I'd actually been was where my lack of pride, shame, unfulfillment, and compromised confidence thrived. The wider the gap that existed between who I know I could be and the way I was living my life in that season, the deeper those feelings of inadequacy presented.

Understanding the problem also gave birth to the solution. The answer to engineering the best possible feelings about myself when I was by myself would be fostered in the creation of *integrity*. Yes, the traditional definition of integrity is important in life: we should all strive for honesty and strong moral principles. But here, the word *integrity* is about alignment. Creating the congruence between who I'd hope to be and how I show up on this day, today, the only day I can control, to close the gap where my struggle thrives.

So, I asked the question that I'll pose to you now:

How do you create integrity in your life that allows you to feel the best about yourself when you're by yourself at the end of a day?

The answer starts with that very clear vision of where you're headed. Who are you hoping to become? It's the motion picture playing in your head of how you hope to feel that day, live into a life of impact, tap fully into your passions, and unlock your purpose in the future.

Whether that vision is three months from now or three years from now, once you have a clear hold on where you're going, you get to reverse engineer how you'll get there by understanding what you'll have to do today to get one step closer. Building the habits and routines, setting the goals, auditing your consumption, surrounding yourself with the resources to allow

How Do I Feel About Myself When I'm By Myself?

LACK OF INTEGRITY

INTEGRITY

WHO I KNOW I CAN BE,
AM MEANT TO BE

HOW I'M SHOWING
UP FOR MY LIFE TODAY

WHO I KNOW I CAN BE,
AM MEANT TO BE

SCARED

NO
CONFIDENCE

UNMOTIVATED

UNFULFILLMENT

PROUD
CONFIDENT
COURAGEOUS
MOTIVATED
FULFILLED

SHAME

HOW I'M SHOWING
UP FOR MY LIFE TODAY

your true self to emerge. All of it coming back to a single question in this pursuit for integrity:

> What conditions in your life would need to be true today to allow that version of you to come alive?

This was the epiphany moment. In retrospect it's such a simple thing that I don't know how I didn't see it earlier. But implementing a practice I started calling "If/Then" in my life has allowed a clear framework for how to build the kinds of habits and routines necessary to achieve my goals. It's the idea that if you want a certain kind of life, if you are interested in your future vision materializing, then you need to do specific things every single day. This is an exercise in intentionality, where the intended outcome is only possible if specific conditions are satisfied.

This is where the rubber meets the road. We're now taking all the work we've done in this book so far and creating a practical list of what it's going to take to help us manifest this vision of who we'd hope to become.

For some, doing the work of knowing what to place on the If/Then worksheet may feel like an overwhelming exercise. You might not yet be connected to some of what you need from an internal motivation perspective to command the answers that you're seeking. I've been there. You are normal. But there are resources that exist to help you step through the exercise in a way that will help you narrow in on the answer.

I recently had a conversation with Steven Kotler, a twelve-time bestselling author, award-winning journalist, and founder of the Flow Research Collective. We talked about the five linear steps that his research has found to be necessary for cultivating the intrinsic motivation required to propel forward with focus and flow.

1. Curiosity: Our most basic motivator, individual and specific to you. When I'm curious about something, I'm naturally apt to pay more attention to it. So, as a foundational building block for motivation, that focus becomes a fuel that keeps me going, usually in a more productive way. We find our passion

when we take this to the next level and begin to identify areas where multiple curiosities collide and overlap.

2. Passion: When our curiosities mature and evolve into passion, we pay even more attention. Like you, when I'm passionate about something, I focus on it in a way that requires little to no incremental brain power. I'm talking about a fierce, deep attentiveness that keeps us engaged and propels us forward. Yes, please.

3. Purpose: You hit a deeper level when you're able to take something you're passionate about and direct it to the service of others. If you do work that focuses on impact, you know the chemical rush you get that makes you feel amazing about the work. Those feelings engender a flow state that keeps you going even further and faster in the pursuit of unlocking and delivering your gifts.

4. Autonomy: This is the freedom to pursue purpose. The research shows that autonomy and attention are coupled systems, the former dependent on the latter. We pay more attention when we are afforded the freedom to drive, own, and lead out on our work. It's why we spent the time we did talking about where our beliefs come from, from whom we seek approval, the rules that we follow so that in freeing ourselves from them, the pursuit of purpose is possible.

5. Mastery: Developing the skills to pursue your purpose well. Through trial and error. Embracing the growth mindset on a never-ending journey of improvement over time.

Running through this linear stack of five steps is the intrinsic motivational foundation that gives way to setting and achieving goals. The tactical work that comes in defining what you have to do every day to get a step closer to where you want to go and who you hope to become.

As I write this book, I am in the midst of doing the work to understand how to go even further in unlocking the gifts that live inside of me. I believe I was put on this planet by a creator with an intention. My drive for self-actualization, this fulfillment of my talent and potential, comes from a desire to honor those gifts; it comes from the hope that my creator will maximize the utility of my talents. For me, this isn't necessarily about the pursuit of abundance or my intention to build a teaching empire or anything else that's material. Rather, it's almost exclusively connected to the way I want to feel about myself when I'm by myself. When I honor this intention by fully tapping into the things that exist inside of me, the possibilities for my life are wildly more expansive and impactful.

What's interesting is that I've also discovered a truth in the books, podcasts, and research on the topic of maximizing potential: the extraordinary feelings of using your gifts, tapping into your passions, and living into your purpose have an equally deep effect on how you feel in a negative way when you don't.

Psychologist Abraham Maslow said, "A musician must make music, an artist must paint, a poet must write, if he is to be ultimately at peace with himself. What a man can be, he must be. This need we may call self-actualization. . . . This tendency might be phrased as the desire to become more and more what one is, to become everything that one is capable of becoming."

Maslow, the godfather of human needs, understood what I've experienced in my life, what I know you've experienced in yours, and what Steven Kotler's research backed up: not unlocking our potential is *bad* for us. Like actually bad. Harvard reports that one in ten adults are depressed, anxiety prescriptions are at an all-time high, and the number of deaths by suicide has overtaken automobile accidents. Understanding the root cause is especially urgent because of the epidemic proportions we're talking about in this day and age.

What the research is telling us loud and clear is that it isn't just past trauma or genetics, but that work that is absent passion, purpose, and the opportunity to unlock your gifts is highly correlated to a mental health crisis. It underscores the mandate to pursue this purpose, if not for the sense of fulfillment and the honor it might bring the intention of your creator, then at a minimum as a means to stave off the anguish and pain that leaving your gifts locked inside ultimately invites.

LOGBOOK

JOURNALING ACTIVITY

If you find yourself to be someone who's struggling with a lack of meaningful work, dive into these questions to see if there is a way to shift your mindset between now and something more meaningful coming along in your career.

- How are the challenging conditions creating opportunities to learn?
- Can you be grateful for what the job affords you?
- Can you find a coach or a mentor to help you build the skills and the confidence that you need?
- Are there ways you can provide value that are different than what you are currently doing or have done in the past?
- Are there ways to work on areas you'll need for the job you want next while you're in this current organization or role?

The decision that sits before you is not so much a choice as a mandate: in the pursuit to feel the way you'd hope to when you're by yourself, you must cultivate the courage to push past fear, you must embrace growth, you must reframe failure, and you must leave behind the suffering you know.

You must leave the harbor.

LOGBOOK

JOURNALING ACTIVITY

So, IF you're going to leave the harbor (and you are), THEN what must you do to step into who you were meant to be?

IF . . . _____

THEN . . . _____

_____

IF . . . _____

THEN . . . _____

_____

IF . . . _____

THEN . . . _____

_____

IF . . . _____

THEN . . . _____

SAY YES

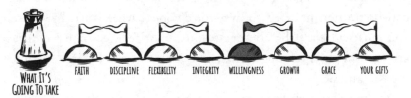

WHAT IT'S GOING TO TAKE | FAITH | DISCIPLINE | FLEXIBILITY | INTEGRITY | WILLINGNESS | GROWTH | GRACE | YOUR GIFTS

Nine months into my career at The Walt Disney Company, I wanted to manufacture an opportunity to give my boss a reason to promote me into a higher-paying, more challenging position. I entered the company as an assistant brand manager in the home video division for the Miramax product, the critically acclaimed independent studio that the company had acquired not long before I arrived. The job was exciting in that it encompassed pricing, packaging, the bonus content that would live on the DVDs, and the occasional reason to interact with the producers or talent involved. My issue was that this piece of the business was a rounding error to the bottom line compared to the animated classics and live action blockbusters that the balance of the company produced through Disney, Pixar, Touchstone, and ABC Studios.

I approached the head of sales at the time and made a pitch. Since I was intimately familiar with the niche product that lived inside of my brand, and the salespeople working in the field were overwhelmingly focused on the rest of the slate that mattered most to their bonuses, I offered to offset their load. My sell was that if I were to go on the sales calls with the major accounts and pitch the product that I knew so well, then his team could keep their focus trained on what mattered most. While they crushed their *vital few*, I'd take care of the *trivial many*.

I hit the road, pitched the product, and landed it while stifling the jazz-hands "ta-da" that it deserved. And it worked. It worked well. It worked so well that two months into this creative solution, I got called up to the executive floor and into the office of the sales head, an incredible mentor of mine named Pat.

After acknowledging the success of this endeavor, he said, "I'm thinking of moving you into the field. A sales job on a national account."

Without taking a beat, I replied, "My answer is yes."

He shook his head and said, "I haven't told you where it is, or what account it is. This would require a move."

Again, without hesitation, "My answer is yes."

Since the accounts included Best Buy, the fourth biggest retail account for the home entertainment division, the destination was Minneapolis. It is among the coldest places on the entire planet. As a Southern California boy who'd gone to Pepperdine University, I'd always lived within five miles of a beach. Had never lived away from my family. Had no experience whatsoever in sales. And at age twenty-seven would be the youngest salesperson on a national account. I'd never lived alone, let alone in a city where I knew not one single person. And yet, my answer, immediately and repeatedly, was "yes."

As Richard Branson said, "If someone offers you an amazing opportunity and you are not sure you can do it, say yes. Then learn how to do it later." That was the plan. It became a part of my personal brand: the guy who agrees to take on something new, even if he doesn't yet know what he's getting into or how to do the thing he's been asked to do. Say yes, then figure out how.

About a year into living in Minnesota, I got a call from Pat's boss, the head of the division at the time and current CEO of The Walt Disney Company, Bob Chapek. Remembering the way I'd jumped at the chance to move, with a year of success in figuring out how to do a job that I hadn't been qualified for, he asked me if I'd consider taking on a new project: an attempt at leveraging technology and the convenience needs of consumers with a DVD that would self-destruct *Mission: Impossible* style and render itself unplayable forty-eight hours after being opened. The plan was to compete with Blockbuster and Netflix with a rental replacement called EZ-D.

I went to my peers in the sales force along with a couple of other mentors in the company to get their opinion on the opportunity that was being presented. Every one of them told me it was a project that was destined to fail, that the path I was on at one of the leading retailers was unbelievably safer, more predictable. Each of them told me that I'd be making a mistake if I left a thing that they each valued so much in status and certainty for the sketchy prospect of launching something new.

So, I weighed their wise counsel, respectfully dismissed it, and immediately said "yes." I agreed to take on this unknown thing because of the person asking. I was willing to move my life again, back to Los Angeles, for the opportunity to be once again thrown into something I knew absolutely nothing about. The past year had afforded extraordinary growth, and more than that, the evidence of my previous "yes" creating new opportunity was the permission necessary to say "yes" again.

That next assignment was tough. Introducing disruptive technology that challenges the status quo, an insurgent approach to the incumbents in the market. It required an entirely new set of muscles, thinking, and strategy. It had my team pushing into new points of distribution in unconventional places like convenience stores, gas stations, pizza delivery, and even prisons. It was exhilarating and frustrating. Exciting and hard. And at the end of the year, as predicted by my peers and mentors, it crashed and burned. A good idea that consumers just weren't ready for.

As we were putting the last nail in the coffin of the project, Bob reached out to ask me if I'd consider reentering the sales force, but this time applying the experiences from my nontraditional EZ-D journey to the very traditional business. In this new role, I'd be developing distribution relationships with retailers who'd never considered selling entertainment, let alone DVDs. I immediately said yes. It started another year of new skill building. A completely different kind of sales approach is required when you're trying to convince someone to consider an entire category before you sell your specific product.

The successes of each of these roles led to the opportunities that would follow for the next decade. By the time I was done, there'd be eleven jobs under thirteen bosses over seventeen years. I wasn't the most qualified candidate for nine of those jobs. I absolutely did not like six of them. But I said yes to all of them, and that decision to say yes, to walk into situations where I had insecurity about my ability to do something new, is what enabled me to go from assistant to president.

My journey after Disney has been cascading RSVPs to an invitation into the unknown. Leaving a twenty-five-year career in entertainment for a start-up entrepreneur journey. Answering the terrifying call to leverage vulnerability in books and coaching. Shouldering the responsibility that comes in the pursuit of impact while weathering the inevitable criticism. All were about listening to the powerful voice of our own intuition, trusting that we might not necessarily understand what we were meant to learn or how we were supposed to grow until long after agreeing to move forward.

I recently heard author Bob Goff say, "God isn't trying to make our lives easier; He wants to make them more meaningful." The meaning that we're looking for in life requires that, on some level, we surrender and choose to trust the journey, especially as it introduces a path that we haven't previously traversed. So often, the things we desire most are delivered only to those who step in the faith of believing they'll be found along the way.

As much as I know it can be scary and triggering and hard, saying yes to the unknown changes the way you believe yourself to be capable of handling the unknown. Walking toward fear is the only way you cultivate courage. Intentionally moving into things that you know will be hard. Reframing how you'll come to see yourself as someone who can do hard things. Going from *thinking you might* to *knowing you can* will change your life forever.

It all starts by saying "yes" to the invitation to step into something new.

LOGBOOK

JOURNALING ACTIVITY

Get to know your intuition. Name it if you have to. The thing that Glennon Doyle might call her Knowing or my pastor might call discernment, it's the gut feeling you have, your deepest instincts bubbling up into your consciousness. Set aside time from your day-to-day and sit with your intuition. Make a relationship with it to understand the insights it's begging you to listen to. Part of courage is trusting this voice when we hear it in a way that allows us to say yes. Once you've gotten to know each other, take out a journal and write down everything you've discovered about what your intuition is trying to tell you.

THE LINEAR JOURNEY AHEAD

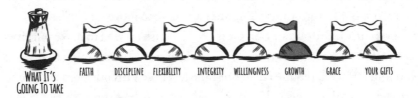

WHAT IT'S GOING TO TAKE — FAITH — DISCIPLINE — FLEXIBILITY — INTEGRITY — WILLINGNESS — GROWTH — GRACE — YOUR GIFTS

The decision to leave the harbor for that lighthouse that sits on the opposite shore in many ways is linear. That is, it is a process that requires you to intentionally move yourself through four distinct environments, in sequential order, to be able to unlock what you're hoping for in a fulfilled life. The broader framework of this entire book was built with an eye to the ways we need to think about courage so that we can effectively navigate from right to left.

Safe Harbor

Many of us find ourselves living in this space. If you've gotten this far in the book, you have some impulse to move away from it for the growth and fulfillment that exists outside of it. Clinging to comfort is a by-product of fear of the unknown, the disbelief in our abilities to acquire new skills, the way we've framed the risks associated with failure, or the illusion of control we convince ourselves we have by "playing it safe." Of course, we've spent many pages discussing the dangers of comfort, the trade-offs that come with choosing to stay in the suffering we know.

John Maxwell said, "The distance between where you stand now and where you want to be is measured by the changes you're willing to make in your life." More than anything, my hope for this book is to equip you with the courage to make change. I want you to connect to the courage and confidence that lives inside of you to take one step after another away from this place you've known for all the opportunity to unleash the purpose and meaning you deserve.

Pool of Fear

Just beyond our safe harbor lies fear. The pool of fear is where our worry of failure, judgment from other people, anxieties about the unknown, and inadequacies dictated from our inner critic thrive. Our fear lives to chip away at our confidence, undermine our self-image, have us questioning our identity and second-guessing our worthiness for the road ahead. Fear sucks. And fear is universal.

Not a single person who's pushed toward fulfillment has escaped the fear zone. There is only one route from comfort to growth, and it travels through the ravine of fear. That ravine is like a moat around a castle; it surrounds comfort on all sides. There is no alternative route. There is no drawbridge, no option of jumping over it or navigating around it. The only way that you'll get to the other side is by plunging right in and pushing straight through.

What it requires is much of what we've talked about in this book. Drawing your fear into the light and assessing what is real and what is imagined. Discarding the imagined; and for those very real fears, building a plan to equip yourself to make this journey. To do it scared, but prepared. It comes with the mandate of reframing your limiting beliefs into empowering stories. Upending the relationship you have with failure as a thing to avoid and turning it into something you see as the only way to learn and grow. As this elegant illustration shows, see it as the *only* route to success. Seeing the feedback that comes from mistakes along the way as the single richest source of intel to help you become who you're hoping to become.

Until you choose to descend into the pool of fear, you will never lose sight of the shore of comfort. You will never leave the suffering you know. You will never see the lighthouse calling you home to fulfillment.

LOGBOOK

JOURNALING ACTIVITY

Challenge Your Fears

I am afraid of failing at _____

Or

I am afraid of being exposed as _____

Now write down all the worst-case scenarios if this fear were realized. Next to each scenario, decide what is the percentage chance of it actually happening.

_____   _____
_____   _____
_____   _____
_____   _____
_____   _____

What is the one thing with the highest-percentage chance of happening? _____

Write five good things that could come out of that most possible scenario:

1. _____
2. _____
3. _____
4. _____
5. _____

Sea of Learning

The sea of learning is as it sounds, the environment inside of which you acquire new skills. By pushing against the boundaries of your comfort, you begin to reframe what you believe yourself to be capable of. In trying new things, the guarantee that you won't get it perfect from the start provides the breadcrumbs to follow to do it better next time. The learning zone is where you find new ways to handle new situations and appreciate the different kind of playbook required now that the game has changed.

When I was running in the past year, I found myself fascinated by the story of Roger Bannister, the first man to break the four-minute mile. Over the course of human history, the thousands of years that people had been running, the feat had never been accomplished. There were stories that running that fast would cause the heart to explode and the general belief that it just wasn't humanly possible. And then one day in 1954, Bannister accomplished the impossible, finishing the mile in 3 minutes and 59.4 seconds. He said that he visualized crossing the finish line at 3:59 so many times that he came to believe with certainty that it was possible.

But to me, the fascinating thing about this story was what happened just after he broke the milestone. Though the feat hadn't ever been accomplished, his record was snapped just forty-six days later by an Australian named John Landy, and has subsequently been accomplished more than 1,400 times. What was it that afforded Landy and these other runners the ability to do a thing that hadn't ever been done before? Some extraordinary development in nutrition or shoes? No. Once they had proof that it was possible, they believed that it was.

The learning zone is where we develop the proof of what's possible for our lives. Putting ourselves intentionally into uncomfortable, less familiar situations for the opportunity to prove that we can survive them. Toil in that friction until we move from survival into skill acquisition, and ultimately from knowing we can do new things to actually beginning a journey toward mastery.

Ocean of Growth

The growth zone is where you start living into your passion, your developed strengths, and the way you were designed to best impact others. As you find a flow in the growth zone, you'll see pieces of your vision come into focus in your day-to-day life; you'll begin developing mastery in areas that light your heart up. Having achieved the foundational goals you set to get you here, the growth zone offers the opportunity to set new, bolder goals that will help you cast a new vision for what the next lighthouse you'll push toward looks like.

It's in the ocean of growth that you'll experience the day in a way that has you feeling the best about yourself when you're by yourself. Your connection to purpose is nurtured here. You'll find yourself continuing to achieve more and more of your goals in a way that builds both confidence and the courage to handle anything that comes your way.

The only way that you can progress through the comfort-to-growth continuum is by staying connected to the work you've done in the If/Then exercise via attention to your health, habits, and routines. Since we've covered health in an earlier chapter, let's turn our focus to habits and routines.

HABITS

I covered the basics of habits in my last book, but again will recommend that you read *Power of Habit* by Charles Duhigg if you haven't already. Duhigg breaks down the science behind the habit loop: there's a *cue* that triggers a *routine* that ultimately delivers a *reward*. The trick is understanding when we're triggered and choosing a healthy routine that will still deliver the reward we're in search of rather than a routine that acts more like a coping mechanism.

For example:

THE CUE

THE ROUTINE

THE REWARD

Bad habit: when I get anxious (cue), I grab a drink (routine) to calm my nerves (reward).

Good habit: when I get anxious (cue), I go for a run (routine) to calm my nerves (reward).

The trigger is the same, the reward is the same, but the response to the trigger is intentionally different. That's how we address bad habits or work to form new ones. As is turns out, much of our habit response is unconscious reflex, so the more we can understand when our cues present themselves, the more likely we are to consciously make a better choice and develop better habits.

In his *New York Times* bestselling book, *Atomic Habits,* James Clear identified the five places to consider when attempting to identify and anticipate triggers:

- Time of day (you snack every night at 9:00 p.m.).
- Location (your anxiety peaks as you pull into your office parking lot).
- Preceding event (you get sad when you see a notification on Facebook from an ex).
- Emotional state (when you're insecure, you have an extra glass of wine).
- Other people (when your mother-in-law walks into Thanksgiving dinner).

The hope is that by understanding the basics of the habit loop and the instances when you're most likely to be triggered that you're able to engineer the habits that support your If/Then statements in a way that accelerates your progression through the comfort-growth continuum.

LOGBOOK

JOURNALING ACTIVITY

For your bad habits, identify when they tend to be triggered. Bringing these into our conscious mind allows us a chance to replace bad routines with good ones.

- *Time.* Meaning the time of day.
- *Location.* There are places for all us that elicit a mindset shift.
- *The immediately preceding action.* This is the thing that happened last.
- *Emotional state.* An emotional-state shift generally triggers a flight-or-fight response.
- *Other people.* Let's be honest, we all have people who trigger us.

But beyond the basics, there are three additional habit hacks that are game changers as you're able to incorporate them in your day-to-day:

- *Keystone Habits.* These are the good habits that if adopted have a spillover effect into other parts of your life or other habits that support your goals. Think committing to regular exercise, a gratitude or meditation practice, frontloading your calendar, or sitting down as a family for dinner. In every instance, each of these are good habits that in and of themselves produce a benefit, but also by nature have a knock-on effect that helps something else in a positive way. For example, moving my body for at least thirty minutes every morning is a really good habit. But it's also a keystone habit because that act has me more considerate around eating foods that bless my body. It provides more energy in my day, boosts my sex drive, and models the importance of staying active for my kids. Keystones deliver many downstream benefits from adopting a single good habit. When building new habits, research and commit to these first.

- *Habit Stacking.* This is simply the idea of adding a new habit just before or just after an existing habit. James Clear describes it as "a special form of implementation intention." In other words, rather than hoping that you'll make a more conscious choice when you're triggered, you build the new habit with intention by attaching it to something you already do regularly. For example, in the midst of training for the Iron Man, I do twenty push-ups after I've gone to the bathroom and before I've washed my hands. Every time. When I make my coffee in the morning, I spend the eight minutes that it brews writing down what I'm grateful for from the day before. Every time. When my alarm goes off in the morning, before I've even turned on a light, I walk into my closet and put on my workout gear and running shoes. Every time.

- *Consistency Compounds.* It may sound like common sense, but the more consistent you are with the habits you commit to, the more impact they'll have and the easier it will be to stay on track. As John Maxwell said, "Your health is the accumulation of your choices, good or bad, over time. If you decide each day to make good choices no matter how seemingly insignificant, those good choices compound as the days pass." Where does a car get its best gas milage? On the highway. Why? Because bodies in motion stay in motion. Because a car already moving that fast requires less energy from an engine to keep it going. Habits work in the same way. When I've been in the garage gym every morning three days in a row, that fourth day is unbelievably easier than the first day after three days off.

Routine

A morning routine is the difference between hoping to have a good day and actively planning for one. My day starts the same way, every day. I do the same things in the same order each morning. I do this because, over time, I have tweaked a formula that works best for engineering how I want to feel, focus, and perform in the day ahead.

- My morning routine starts the night before. Getting to bed at the same time every night, to afford the amount of sleep I know I need to have the energy I need to show up well for myself, my kids, and my team.
- I wake up at the same time each morning (do not hit snooze).
- I get into my workout clothes,
- brew my coffee,
- work through my gratitude,
- take my vitamins with a green juice.
- I then take my coffee to the back patio where I pray and enjoy a moment of peace.
- I then set the intention for my day by looking at my calendar and identifying the most important things I need to accomplish, making sure they happen first, then the second most important, and so on.
- I head out to the garage gym to work out
- before coming back in to get the kids up for school,
- make three boring eggs for me, get breakfast going for the kids,
- get the kids out the door to school
- before jumping in the shower to start my day.

This is what my morning looks like. Every morning. I am a cyborg about it happening at the same time and in the same order so that it isn't something I need to think about or negotiate. And just because it works for me does not mean that this should be your morning routine. In developing this over time, I've found that you need a routine that satisfies five basic conditions that are unique to you:

1. Consistency. You need to build a routine that you can do every single day. A routine that's built around the intricacies and chaos of your life, the demands of your job, the needs of your family.

2. Attainability. Your routine has to be something that realistically meets you where you are. If you've never risen at dawn, run long distance, or read nonfiction, you can't build a routine that immediately has you doing all three. You'll end up oversleeping, with blisters, and a headache. Know where you are and allow your routine to evolve over time.

3. Relevance. The routine you create must serve the vision of who you're becoming. It has to align with your personal values, your If/Then statements, and your "why." If you build a routine based on someone else's values or something that's disconnected from the pursuit of your calling, it won't last. Relevance keeps your routine more important than your excuses.

4. Flexibility. I know I said you have to build a routine that you can do every day, but life doesn't actually work like that. Find a way to build a routine that with a practice like Sunday-evening frontloading can have you calling an audible on a Thursday morning when one of your kids has a doctor's appointment and it pushes your morning run on the track to evening yoga in the den.

5. Simplicity. If you overcomplicate your routine, you will not stick to it. Develop something with as little wind resistance as possible. Find ways to eliminate the way that uncontrollable variables (weather, time change, school starting) could upend the plan that you create.

There we have it. As you prepare to cast off from the harbor, consider this linear sequence of moving from comfort, through fear, to the learning that produces growth. Once we come to understand the sequence, then it's time to apply action. Planning is nothing without action, and the action required comes in the form of how we tend to our health and build the right kinds of habits and routines. The way we put those plans into play should inform how we hope to show up today in a way that gets us one step closer each day to the vision of who we're becoming. You know what to do. Let's go.

LOGBOOK

JOURNALING ACTIVITY

Take a dive into the habits that aren't currently supporting the vision of who you'd hope to become. Creating self-awareness for the areas to challenge or replace existing bad habits is where developing good habits starts.

- What habits in your life aren't supportive of your goals?
- What habits are sabotaging your progress?
- What habits need to be changed to better serve you and/ or your family?
- What habits could be added to your life to reduce stress, build confidence, and promote health?

THE NONLINEAR JOURNEY AHEAD

I wish I could tell you that if you just follow the sequence and build the right routine that every day will be better than the last. But that's not how life works. This journey is also nonlinear in that you're going to have a string of good days that are followed by a bad one. The way you react to failure in trying something new, the temptation to keep people happy as you set new boundaries, the battles you'll face with that voice inside your head, and a slew of other things will introduce discomfort that throws you off, challenges your motivation, and has you second-guessing whether you've got what it takes to make it to the other shore.

In those early days working in a start-up environment, over the course of a week, we'd go from celebrating the sellout of a conference to lighting our hair on fire because of a shipping snafu with our journals. Highs met with lows. Progress met with failure. Over the long arc of time, there was success through learning and growth, but that success was all over the board day-to-day. In his bestselling book, *Creative Calling*, Chase Jarvis illustrated the roller coaster that starting any project goes on: a fluctuating joy/pain continuum over time.

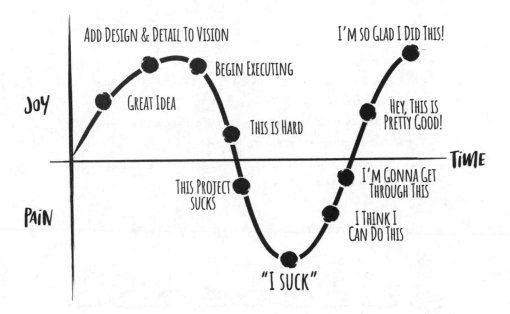

This is a pretty fair representation of how the experience of anything new is going to feel. Encouraged to jump until being confronted by new challenges that have you questioning everything. But the willingness to stay with it when it gets hard allows you to turn the corner where learning, skill acquisition, and ultimately mastery produce the wins that you stack on each other to build momentum.

I know in my own grief journey after the end of my marriage, the processing of all the emotions that come in change would see a string of good days followed by a really hard one, often out of the blue. One week in particular I can remember signing the deal for this very book and another deal for a children's book based on the Tea Time I have with my daughter, Noah. In the midst of feeling like I could see a vision for my future where one had previously been harder to connect to, a single phone call brought me to my knees. A simple, amicable, technical question about how we'd handle splitting time with the kids prompted a four-hour crying session.

A younger me would have tried to push those feelings away. Tried to white-knuckle, shake myself out of it, and tough-talk myself into being strong, hard, or whatever. Now I just let the feelings come on down like they're a contestant on *The Price Is Right*. Sit with them. Try to understand what role they believe they're here to play and how they might help me get back up.

Contrary to what you may see on social media where most people are representing that everything's good all the time, there's no reality in that. Reality is good and hard. Real life is a nonlinear experience where struggle and progress coexist, where hard days show up like unexpected out-of-town guests. Experiencing those hard days doesn't make me weak or less, it makes me human. Just like you.

What I have perspective for now is that when we experienced a customer service crisis and it felt like the world was ending, our response to it and the work we did to rebuild the trust with customers we'd let down actually forged stronger relationships and better processes and systems in the company. What I appreciate now is that in that week when I found myself crying for the better part of the day, it was still a fantastic week, full of things to celebrate, opportunities that excited me, conversations that filled my soul, and experiences that made me believe in the guarantee of the extraordinarily good things ahead.

This journey requires that you hold the idea that good days and bad, wins and losses, highs and lows all exist. On the whole, you'll stack more wins over time, learn more from the bad beats, and find yourself evolving in the growth zone, so long as you're able to get back up and keep going on the days when life pulls the rug out from under you.

The habits and routines that you'll set aren't for the good days. They're there to keep you going on the hard days. They're there to get you back on the boat when unexpected swells throw you overboard. Being thrown from the ship isn't the issue. In fact it's a guarantee. If you've truly moved away from comfort and are pushing yourself to learn, then it will happen. The speed with which you get back on board and get hold of the helm before it steers itself toward the rocks is what matters most. It's why hacking your motivation is so important when we're promised that the price of entry here is having hard days.

Hacking Your Motivation

People always ask me how I stay so motivated. The simple answer is, I don't. Like the rest of you, I struggle regularly to feel like doing the things I know I need to do for the life I want to have. So how do I handle the days when I don't feel like it? I just do it anyway. I do it anyway by staying connected to some simple hacks that have helped me get back up or keep on going when the feeling to do so wanes:

- *Positivity:* It begins with what you surround yourself with to keep you feeling positive. Develop a daily gratitude practice. Exclusively follow optimistic influences on social media. Be careful not to overconsume the news, whose business model is fear. Guard the walls of your mind and your thoughts in a way that manufactures hopefulness rather than the overwhelm of the moment.
- *Connect to your vision:* It can be a fancy vision board, it can be writing in a journal, it can be Pinterest, whatever Pinterest is, but you have to actually have your vision in a place that you can access on hard days. Reread it. Look at the pictures you've saved. Spend time in the intricacies of the specific detail of this life you're working toward. The reminder of why you're choosing discomfort acts as a catalyst to keep going.
- *Revisit your goals:* Motivation tends to struggle when the goals we've set are either unrealistic relative to our current circumstance in life (see *attainable* in SMART goals), or are no longer connected to the evolving vision of where we're heading now that we're in the midst of the journey (see *relevant*). Your reason for choosing discomfort has to be stronger than your excuses, and that only remains the case if your goals still have relevance in propelling you toward your destination.

- *Diagnose inconsistency:* Get honest about what parts of your daily routine you're having the hardest time being consistent with. Your morning needs to act as a springboard for the day you want to have, irrespective of the conditions that are presented in that day. But that launchpad is only effective if it's something you can commit to religiously. So, if there are circumstances in your life that compromise your ability to do something regularly, adjust your routine.

- *One day at a time:* The weight of the conditions we find ourselves in can be overwhelming because of what feels like a never-ending Groundhog Day. When you can train your focus to the routine that it's going to take to get through today, and only today, without worrying about what happens next, how long it's going to take to return to feeling *normal*, you give yourself a fighting chance. The only thing you can actually control is how you show up today. Worrying about the uncontrollable future is wasted energy and unnecessary weight that stifles motivation. If the full day is too much to contemplate, consider blocking time throughout your day. What's the next right thing you need to do to make it to lunch? What's the next right thing to make it to dinner?

- *Celebrate your progress:* An unfortunate human trait is to focus on what we didn't accomplish rather than what we did. How much farther we have to go rather than how far we've come. So, celebrate and consider how you reward hitting small milestones along the way to actually feel it. Schedule it in your calendar if you have to, because intentionally pausing to develop pride in your progress will act as fuel to keep going.

- *Give yourself some grace:* Last one, best one. There's a trap we all find ourselves in when it comes to motivation, and that's comparing ourselves to other people's progress. Sizing up how much more motivated they seem to be. But you are not on their journey; you are on your own. Though they may be presenting a curated view of having it all together and crushing it every day, trust me, they do not. If, like you, they're pursuing something that really matters, they struggle and doubt and have overboard moments just like I do and just like you will. When you have a hard day, connect to having done the best you could in the conditions you're in. Take a breath, focus on some self-care, and give yourself a healthy serving of grace.

To the final point, *rest and recovery* is as or more important than *hustle and grind*. You cannot work hard enough to make this process linear. You can't hustle your way to preempting bad days. The cultural narrative that celebrates hustle tends to do so in a way that makes grace, rest, and self-care a thing that we feel badly for indulging in. Grace, rest, and self-care are not an indulgence, they are not selfish; they are, however, mandatory requirements in this journey ahead.

And beyond that, there's a temptation to think of how good we'll feel once we find our purpose. After we move away from comfort. The day we're finally out of debt or get that promotion or hit a number on a scale. Or anything else. The idea that you're holding out for *someday* to feel peace, joy, and a sense of fulfillment is a dangerous trap. Psychologist Robert Holden coined the term *destination addiction* to describe this. It creates a troubling unconscious connection in your brain that if you can work hard enough you can feel worthy. That once you get *there* you'll be lovable, to someone else or yourself. These are the thoughts that are particularly strong on the down days in the nonlinear journey.

I was having a conversation with Ben Rector about his song "Peace," the second most-played song on my patio of the same name behind his "Sailboat" in my hardest and best year ever. I asked him about these lines from the song:

I used to worry about the future, but the future never came
Tried living in the past, but it never did quite feel the same
I used to think that there was a place I would rather be
But I got there enough times to realize that
You are only ever here

He said, "In the hustle culture, the thing that's being sold is 'if you can just find what you're passionate about and what your dream is and then do it, *then* you'll be happy,' and I just want to run out into the streets and say, 'That's not true. Get good at being happy where you are because that's the only place you're ever going to be.'"

This entire book is trying to equip you with the courage to find your passion, visualize your dream, to push into fear to actually do it. But it also feels important to drive home the point that the mandate doesn't mean that when you arrive at your destination you will find your peace, connect to a sense of pride, or experience fulfillment. You do not need to wait until then. You cannot wait until then. You are only ever going to be where you are, so you have to find a way to connect to the feelings you're hoping for *then* in the *here and now*.

The song ends with my favorite lines:

Through the ups and downs
I have figured out you find peace where you make it
Scenery won't change it
And I wasted so much time
Thinking I could ever find enough of anything
That would bring me peace

Peace is where you make it. Joy is where you find it in 143 small things every day. Evidence of the gifts you have to be grateful for exist today so long as you look for them. In this nonlinear journey of becoming, don't wait to experience the good inside the struggle. We'll only ever be here. Manufacture the mindset to receive the good that already exists, and you'll have all you need for the ups, the downs, and whatever comes your way next.

A few months into my divorce, I had an idea for a podcast. In figuring out "next," writing books, online coaching, and the *Rise Together* podcast were my primary focus. And since it was just the week before the d-word was brought up in my house that I'd read about hers, I reached out to fitness and transformation expert Heidi Powell to see if she'd be willing to come on the *Rise Together* show so we could talk about the emotions of a relationship coming to an end, single parenting, and starting over.

As much as we knew each other from the endorsement she'd given my first book and a handful of random notes about building a company, we'd never met. I didn't really expect she'd be up for talking, let alone about divorce. But as it turned out, she was coming through Texas from Arizona just days after my note, and she agreed to talk.

As much as she is incredibly beautiful and has a reputation for being bighearted, neither do her justice in person. But this wasn't about that. I wasn't looking for someone to date. I honestly was barely eating, running twelve miles a day, in therapy or prayer, and *not* thinking about ladies.

We sat down to start the interview and I couldn't get a sentence out without crying. After thirty minutes of blubbering, I asked if she was ready to hit record, to which she laughed. I was clearly not in a place to have a conversation for the show.

We sat and talked for four hours. Ran through all the similarities in our divorces that chose us. We each have four kids, were transitioning away from partners we'd been working with, had to work through a relationship ending in public. It made me feel normal.

Over the year that followed, texts gave way to longer texts, which gave way to long phone calls. Netflix at night. Virtual church on Sunday. Months in, the most unexpected thing in the most unexpected time led to a dinner and for the first time in eighteen years, a first kiss.

At a time when I couldn't find it myself, peace found me. Hope came in human form when a woman named Heidi agreed to a podcast that was never recorded. The nonlinear journey of *becoming* got an assist from an acquaintance who'd become more than a friend. Where it leads, only time will tell. For now, I simply consider myself grateful that she came along when she did in this roller coaster called life.

LOGBOOK

JOURNALING ACTIVITY

Celebrate your success. Take a moment to create a list of all that you've accomplished in the past year. Big things and small, any progress in this journey is worthy of being recognized. Take a victory lap—you deserve it.

FINDING YOUR WHY

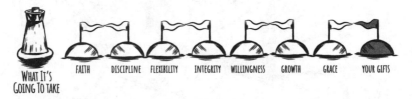

WHAT IT'S GOING TO TAKE — FAITH — DISCIPLINE — FLEXIBILITY — INTEGRITY — WILLINGNESS — GROWTH — GRACE — YOUR GIFTS

As we head for the home stretch in this book, the final, and one of the most important pieces necessary for your success, is establishing your "why." Your North Star. The intention of your creator. Your purpose on this earth. The deep, meaningful thing that you can connect to every single day to keep you moving toward the vision of who you'd hope to become.

Your "why" is the cornerstone of all that you do. It's your calling, your driving force, your passion. The thing that motivates you to get out of bed every day and get it done. Simon Sinek introduced this concept in his books *Start with Why* and *Find Your Why*, and finding your "why" has since become part of our cultural lexicon. As much as zeroing in on your "why" acts as a map to unlocking your purpose and ultimately fulfillment, the trouble for me was that I started really looking for it amidst a midlife funk around forty. And I couldn't find it. I mean, you can only use your "why" as an internal compass and motivation hack if you can identify it. And for a while, I couldn't.

It turns out that I'm not the only one. In the time that I have been doing this work, the single question that I am asked most often is, *What should I do if I can't find my "why"?* It's something I've coached at length about in the courses that live on MrDaveHollis.com and also is part of my last book, *Get Out of Your Own Way*. More than anything, people want to know what to do if they don't already know their purpose. If they can't figure out what they're supposed to be doing with their lives.

In my search for "why," I had to start with this question:

Why don't you already know your true calling?

What makes finding our "why" so elusive for many of us? In my experience, the answer lies in four common *blocks* that prevent you from seeing your "why" clearly and giving yourself the permission to chase it:

- Your skepticism
- Your mindset
- Your identity
- Your needs

Let's break them down.

Your Skepticism

You may be skeptical that a "why" even exists for you. You may think that some people have a clear calling and others don't. That some people are *chosen*, and others are just there to support their climb.

That's not how this works.

We all have a "why." This is not something to be skeptical of. Your "why"—your passion, your calling—does exist. To discover it, you have to start with an open mind. You have to accept that you have been given a unique skill set from the creator of the universe. You have been given something that this world needs. You must believe that your uniqueness is a gift, and that the responsibility that goes along with your gift is an obligation to share what you've been given. To gift the world with your gifts. And your "world" may be specific to the inhabitants of your home or broadly considerate of the population of the entire planet. That's for you to decide.

It's easy to become resigned to dissatisfaction with life. To convince yourself that *maybe this is as good as it gets* or *I'm unlucky and I just have to accept my lot in life*. But we must recognize that these are limiting beliefs. If you find yourself thinking this way, you are going to have to actively rewrite your narrative. You can't discover your "why" if you start your journey with a story of what's *not* possible for you, thinking you're a person destined for a life that's only as good as it is today.

You must believe with every fiber of your being that your calling comes with the responsibility of chasing it down, unlocking it, and allowing it to be something that can impact this world.

Your Mindset

Pushing past skepticism and doubt is the first step in activating the *mindset* you'll need to succeed in this hunt. You need to fully embrace growth if you want to get to your "why." In my previous book I talked about the difference between having a "fixed mindset" and a "growth mindset." You must adopt the latter in order to recognize and move toward your calling. This growth mindset is a must-have ingredient in the courage you're trying to cultivate. By rewiring the way you think about growth, you can and will develop the courage to face the challenges ahead in unlocking your true calling.

As a refresher, "growth" versus "fixed" mindset was developed by psychologist Carol Dweck. According to Dweck, a person with a fixed mindset believes that our intelligence and abilities are a set point, whereas a person with a growth mindset believes that these same traits can be developed over time. Someone with a growth mindset is more open to embracing, rather than avoiding, challenges, and sees them as opportunities. This person will persist through obstacles rather than give up. Which is precisely why cultivating a growth mindset is a prerequisite for finding your calling.

As someone recovering from a fixed mindset, I can tell you that if you have a fixed mindset while you hunt for your calling, your deterministic view of the world will limit what you believe and what you can achieve

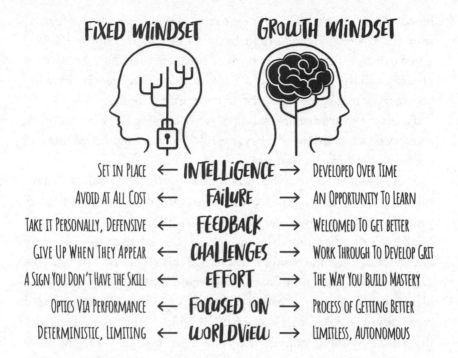

Set in Place ←	**INTELLIGENCE** →	Developed Over Time
Avoid at All Cost ←	**FAILURE** →	An Opportunity To Learn
Take it Personally, Defensive ←	**FEEDBACK** →	Welcomed To get better
Give Up When They Appear ←	**CHALLENGES** →	Work Through To Develop Grit
A Sign You Don't Have the Skill ←	**EFFORT** →	The Way You Build Mastery
Optics Via Performance ←	**FOCUSED ON** →	Process of Getting Better
Deterministic, Limiting ←	**WORLDVIEW** →	Limitless, Autonomous

because you will remain locked in fear. Without the courage that comes in the growth mindset, your calling will remain hidden from you.

Your Identity

Once you accept that you're worthy of a calling, and once you adopt the mindset necessary to chase it, the next obstacle you will have to push through is resistance around *identity*. The identity you have assumed for yourself, and maybe more important, the identity you believe is necessary to be *right* in the eyes of those you've assigned as voices of authority. Unlocking your calling will require a tough reconciliation between who you are deep down and who you believe you need to be.

When you're struggling with identity and its impact on your calling, you may find that you have (consciously or subconsciously) prioritized an identity that's familiar over the one you need to cultivate in order to actively pursue your "why." Toward the end of my time working as the head of sales at The Walt Disney Company, I was struggling internally to find my true calling. I knew that my corporate role was not in line with my broader "why." It was difficult for me to consider an identity that departed from the expectations and external values I had always known. I'd been raised to believe that being a "good man" meant having a big job with a lot of responsibility and a fancy title. But I had to shatter those limiting beliefs in order to take the necessary steps toward my future.

Finding your true calling will involve challenging the way you think about two factors around identity: the role you play for other people and the role society expects you to play.

As a human interacting with other humans, you have assumed certain roles in your relationships. Partner, parent, caretaker, sibling. Whatever your role may be in any given relationship, you have often assumed this role *for other people* rather than for yourself. That other-oriented identity can create blinders to chasing your calling. This is because you may perceive that there is a central conflict, an impossibility in maintaining this identity while chasing your true purpose. When the voice in our head convinces us that standing in our truth is selfish. When our insecurities that unlocking our unique gifts may come at the expense of keeping other people comfortable. As we worry that listening to our intuition may challenge the expectations and standards to which society holds us.

It often comes back to an inability to see the power and possibility of *both*. That you can do something for you and still be present for them. That you as your true, full, fulfilled self is actually the version of you the collective *they* will look up to and get more from. It's because of the light that burns in you. As someone who left a career filled with status for a calling filled with impact, though the former was easy to explain at a dinner party, the latter is the one that's filled my cup. I didn't believe I could pursue this unconventional line of work because I worried that people might think me crazy for leaving certainty for fulfillment. But the ability to hold both purpose and freedom from what other people think has been life altering.

For a woman rowing against the current of patriarchal norms, it may be drowning in "mommy guilt," struggling to believe you can be a good wife and mother while still pursuing a career. For a man against the backdrop of society's definition of masculinity, this might be challenging the idea that *there's no way I can be a good leader if I am vulnerable at work*. In every case, you can be both.

If you are buying into a narrative that is preventing you from seeing and chasing your "why," I can say this as a dedicated father who also pursues his passion: that story is true only if you decide to believe it. Yes, it requires the work we did around personal values, the guardrails required to preserve them, and the reframing of limiting beliefs. The stories we tell to keep us from moving forward are ropes that tether us to the dock until we decide they no longer exist.

Beyond your identity in relationships with others, there is also the issue of how societal expectations can affect your identity. The conversation earlier around what a *real man* or *good girl* would do. What a *good Christian*, *true friend*, or *decent mom* would do. Buying into societal expectations is another way of accepting other people's limits on what's possible for you.

The roles you play for others, and the roles that society expects? They exist and they're not going anywhere. But whether or not you buy into these expectations is actually a choice you get to make. Will it ruffle people's feathers when you reject these limits? Sure. But your "why" is more important.

You must decide: Can you embrace the truth that you can be both? That you can be a good parent while pursuing your career? That you can challenge someone else's definition of conventional to unlock your passion? Can you depart from some of what you believe you have to be in your relationships in order to fulfill your purpose? If you can, your identity won't be the thing standing between you and your calling.

Your Needs

Once you push your skepticism aside, shift your mindset, and make peace with your identity, it's time to address your *needs*. If you don't have a handle on your basic human needs, you won't feel like you have permission to chase your calling.

How do we define needs? One of the most well known explanations is psychologist Abraham Maslow's hierarchy of needs, which you've probably seen before. Maslow depicts our needs as a pyramid, with our physiological needs at the base. We're talking about food and water, warmth and rest. This level is about asking the most basic questions: Am I getting enough sleep? Am I choosing foods that fuel my body? The basic physical foundation you'll need to chase anything. The next level is about safety and security. If you're in a position where you don't feel safe and secure, pursuing something like your "why" at an elevated level may seem unattainable. From there, there are three additional levels that progress to "self-actualization" at the top of the pyramid.

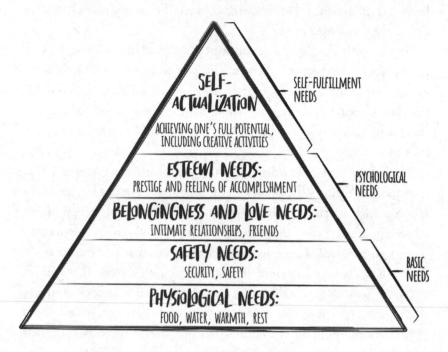

The bottom line? If you want to chase the needs at the top of the pyramid, where fulfillment lives and your "why" is found, you must start with satisfying the basics.

Criteria for Finding Your Why

Once you identify the blocks that may be keeping you from finding your calling, you can turn your attention to actually finding it. Of the hundreds of sources that have tried to describe the components in this elusive hunt, *ikigai*, a Japanese concept that translates to "reason for being," is the one I've most related to in my life. The ideas here are about the intersection between purpose and fulfillment and the way that our actions, when focused in the right space, can give us a sense of meaning in our lives.

Akihiro Hasegawa, a professor at Toyo Eiwa University and a leading researcher in his field, said that *ikigai* is the "feeling that one is alive here and now, and the individual awareness that drives him or her to survive." It's our "why." Our reason for being.

Here, there are the four basic criteria for identifying your "why":

1. *Passion.* It sets your heart on fire.
2. *Mastery.* It's something you're great at.
3. *Impact.* It brings needed light to the world.
4. *Sustenance.* It can create financial security for you.

Let's dig deeper into each of these four categories:

- *Passion.* When trying to pinpoint what lights you up, ask yourself the following questions: When you were a child, what did you love to do? Before you became a parent, a partner, or a leader, how did you spend your spare time? If you had no obligations to other people, what would you be doing? What makes you curious?
- *Mastery.* In order to pinpoint your areas of mastery, ask yourself the following questions: What do you feel most confident doing? When do your innate talents shine brightest? What skills that you've developed make you proud? Where do your skills shine most?
- *Impact.* For this category, ask yourself the following questions: What could you offer to the world that would help and inspire others? How do your strengths fill a need that exists in your circle/family/community/world? Are there ways in which you feel you could contribute to society that you aren't currently exploring?
- *Sustenance.* Last but not least comes sustenance or financial security. Unless you're independently wealthy, pursuit of your "why" must also align with your ability to support yourself and your family. So ask yourself: What are my financial responsibilities? What opportunities exist that I can get paid

for to meet those needs? Are there paid roles that tap into my passion, competencies, and ability to impact others?

LOGBOOK

JOURNALING ACTIVITY

Take out a piece of paper and divide it into four quadrants, each labeled with one of the four preceding categories. Now do a brain dump. Under each category, write down every single thing that applies for you.

PASSION

Lights your heart on fire

COMPETENCY

You're great at it

IMPACT

Brings light to the world

SUSTENANCE

Creates financial security

Now take a look at the lists in each of your four quadrants. Are there items that you've listed in all four? If not, what about three out of four? Or maybe the best you can do is a pursuit that ticks off two of the categories for you. That's okay! This is your starting point.

Let's say you've listed a pursuit under "Passion" and "Impact," but it doesn't seem to fall under "Mastery" and "Sustenance" for you. Or at least not yet. The next step is to ask yourself additional questions about this pursuit in order to determine what additional skills or training you'd need to become great at it and how you could make money at it. This gets you on the path toward finding a pursuit that will sit in all four categories for you.

Something that ticks all four categories is the goal. If you're not good at something yet, but have the other three, this calling won't work until you acquire the skills. If you can't make money doing it yet, but you have the other three, it very well may be your calling, but may be unsustainable until you figure out the business model. For me, the only nonstarter is if you're not passionate about something but have the other three, because passion is harder to manufacture over time. Either you're passionate about something or you're not. In the end, your mission is to find something that checks all four boxes, or you likely don't have something that's strong enough to become your life's calling.

I am passionate about speaking and writing, teaching and reporting. My primary intention with books, coaching, and podcasts is to impact people in ways that might afford them a better life. I happen to be good at this work, a product of years and years of trial and error, my own coaching and feedback. And it turns out that the work is something that allows me to provide financially for my family. In having found a pursuit that connects to each of the four categories, I have 100 percent absolute certainty that I am doing the work of fulfilling my purpose on this planet.

You've probably heard of a Venn diagram, which shows how circles representing different elements overlap with one another. In pursuit of finding your "why," we're looking for the place where the four criteria overlap. That's where you'll find your most authentic self, connect more fully to your purpose, and experience the peace that comes by fulfilling the intention of your creator.

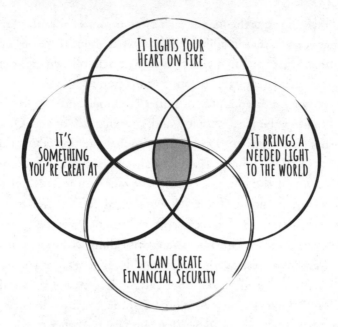

Okay, but what if you're still struggling to figure it out?

What if, after running through these criteria, you're still stuck? That does not make you broken; it makes you human. Give yourself some grace, then tap into the wide array of tools that exist to help you get unstuck. The great news for you is that many tools exist to help you understand how your innate strengths paired with your personality type affect what you are passionate about. If you're having a hard time zeroing in on what you're great at, I recommend taking a diagnostic test like StrengthsFinder to help you zero in on your unique capabilities. If you're hung up trying to figure out what might light a person like you on fire, completing a personality diagnostic like a DiSC or the Enneagram test could be the trick. If you're stuck on what kind of jobs are out there that align with your passion and skills, make friends with LinkedIn and Indeed and the countless other career sites to familiarize yourself with what exists in the market.

And if you're like I was, challenged to know what you're even passionate about, there's hope here too. I enlisted a book called *The Passion Test: The Effortless Path to Discovering Your Life Purpose* where authors Janet Bray Attwood and Chris Attwood delve into a list of questions to help you narrow in on what you could pursue. The questions include:

- What did you dream of when you were a kid?
- What kind of book or movie could you not pass up?
- If you played hooky for a week, what would you do with all that free time?
- What do you really enjoy that most people don't know about you?
- What are you the go-to person for among your friends?
- If you could have your very own how-to show, what would it be about?
- If you won first prize in a talent show, what would it be for?

If you ask those questions, and your answers surprised you or would surprise others, you're onto something.

You've Found Your Why. What's Left to Get in Your Way?

Unfortunately, many things. We bring them up here as we prepare to leave the harbor so that we create the awareness of what to keep an eye out for while cultivating the courage to face each obstacle in this mission of *becoming*. To be successful, you'll have to decide over and over, every day, to push past each of these when they inevitably come up.

- *Other people.* The people in your life have grown accustomed to who you are and how you show up in their lives. Your decision to chase this next version of you may be disruptive for them. Some might not be supportive. And even your cheerleaders will need to take a step back and learn to let you do your thing. You will need to decide what's more important to you: fully embracing your potential or keeping everyone in your life comfortable. Because you can't do both.
- *The work it takes.* Even when pursuing something you love that is impactful, that you're great at, and that can make you money, the process will require work. Sometimes people think that if they can only find their passion, the rest will be easy. Again, not the way it works. Change is hard, and changing your life

will be one of the hardest, and the best, things you've ever done. Buckle up.

- *The time it takes.* You will need to discard the notion that things will simply click into place after a certain amount of time. Instead, think of pursuing your passion as a never-ending journey. Embracing a growth mindset means accepting that you are forever at work on unleashing the possibilities of your passion. Perpetual improvement is the goal.

- *Your relationship to comfort.* Discomfort has been the single greatest catalyst for growth in my life. If you are comfortable where you are, you are not growing. Whether discomfort arrives in confronting your fears over whether you'll succeed in the pursuit of your passion, or the incredibly normal insecurity triggered by new challenges, getting comfortable with discomfort is a prerequisite for progress.

CONCLUSION

YOU MADE IT. Forty-five chapters later, you're here and hopefully feeling equipped with the courage to step into who you've been placed on this planet to be. The true, full, wonderful, weird, bold, unique version of you who feels deeply connected to your passion, your skills, and your ability to impact others. If you're not there yet, have the courage to believe that you'll get there over time and that the work that you've begun has you closer than you've ever been.

As I write this book, I stand proud of who I've become in my past five years of massive change, having made three significant voyages from my safe harbor into the chaotic and choppy seas where growth would forge this best version of me. The discomfort of leaving behind what I knew well was the invitation to become something greater through the challenges of acclimating to something new. Clearly seeing the correlation between leaning into the friction of discomfort and the benefits that came from evolving into this best version of myself has afforded me confidence. Now I can be even more courageous in pushing beyond the boundaries of my comfort zone any time something new begins to feel like something normal.

Three big, life-altering harbor departures in what happened to be two-year cycles.

Back in 2014, Jen Hatmaker's book *Interrupted* begged a simple significant question: What would it mean to interrupt your good life for the possibility of something far greater? In a world where I had so much to be grateful for and comfortable with, where Rachel ran a budding business, I had a thriving career, and we were raising three healthy, happy boys, the seed planted by that question grew into an internal voice that became louder and louder. That intuition that you often bat away became something that could no longer be ignored. For us, it was the call into adoption and the opportunity to complete our family with a daughter.

The year 2016 saw the end of a years-long adoption journey that went through a failed attempt internationally in Ethiopia, the beautiful and traumatic experience of the foster care system, and the ultimately successful private adoption of our daughter, Noah. It required inviting discomfort, intermittent chaos, blood-boiling frustration, and bring-you-to-your-knees grief to step toward the knowledge that our family wasn't yet complete. It required more courage than we knew ourselves to possess on the hardest days. And that happy ending I alluded to earlier in the book was only possible because of the willingness to keep moving through the valleys of fear that heeding this call would require.

Answering the call does not afford you a vote in the conditions you'll face along the way. In fact, what I've come to appreciate is that the conditions themselves are in many ways the reason for answering in the first place. The experience of 2016 was a primer. To show me how strong I could be for having to be so strong. Defining for me what resilience actually is for having to get back up so many times, even on the days when it felt impossible to connect to hope. The circumstances of that incredibly difficult year aren't something that I ever want to relive, but I do have an overwhelming amount of gratitude for what that struggle gifted me in grit, faith, tenacity, a reframed sense of how much I could handle, and the preparation needed to even consider leaving the harbor again. That the choice to choose interruption, to leave the safe harbor at the expense of comfort, produced so much beauty and growth was the evidence my intuition used to assure me that I could be courageous again.

Noah was born at the end of February of 2017. Just two weeks later, I heard that whisper again. Well, the whisper had existed for some time but

I'd been distracted by adventure and the ending of a saga. It was during an evening in the spa with my boys. We had a tradition. They could ask me anything. Sawyer innocuously asked, "What is your biggest fear?" Out of my mouth fell, "not living up to my potential." The whisper became a scream. It was no coincidence that three days later I sat staring at a piece of paper that would forever change my life.

In a world where I had always been wired for certainty, thought the maintenance of comfort was my primary role as a husband and father, clung feverishly to the trappings of predictability even at the expense of my own growth, signing an employment contract had always been my dream. The deal I'd signed three years earlier was cause for celebration, an affirmation in some ways of the nearly two decades of effort, sacrificing time with my family, learning from a lot of mistakes, and saying yes to countless unconventional jobs. Back then, I was still out of my depth, growing through the challenges of a job beyond my competency or experience. But in the eighteen months before this latest deal was placed in front of me, things changed.

The unprecedented leverage afforded by the acquisition of Lucasfilm and Marvel Studios converged with me getting a handle on the learning curve as head of sales in a way that made the job something that was no longer uncomfortable. Yes, it was still an amazing job with extraordinary people and all the benefits that came with its access. But it was no longer a role that required the full use of my potential. In the absence of discomfort, there was no growth. And with no growth, particularly as I was crossing this midlife milestone entering my forties, it left me unfulfilled, unmotivated, and stuck.

The morning in mid-March when a new four-year contract to continue working at everyone else's dream job was placed in front of me, it was the low point of my professional career. Get out the world's smallest violin. I get it. But the ropes that had me docked in a safe harbor of comfort would be reinforced with bigger, stronger, longer-term ties with a single pen stroke. So yes, I appreciate that it can sound tone deaf to complain about getting an extension on a job that was going to provide for my family. But I'll ask for your grace and willingness to see the broader point. The screaming voice of my intuition went into a panic, begging me to reject certainty.

To fight to muster the courage to leave a job that nobody leaves for a life that fewer experience. That I might actually honor the intention of my creator, opt for challenge in the choice for discomfort, and effectively deliver the way I want to feel about myself when I'm by myself. That I might actualize the full use of the gifts that live inside me.

After months of laboring through the feelings of being stuck and sinking deeper into a funk that had me feeling and showing up like the worst version of myself, I went on a trip to Austin, Texas. An exploratory trip with Rachel to just see what life could be like in a world where that contract didn't exist, if I were to leave the stuck that I knew and we started something scary and bold and new. After dinner with Austinite Jen Hatmaker, that question from her book that started the last journey into the unknown was back: What would it mean to interrupt your good but not great life?

The next morning we had a real estate agent drive us around to see the different neighborhoods around town. As we drove into the driveway of the home from which I'm currently writing these words, I let the voice speak out loud. "We need to make the leap." In real time we started to figure out the financing and the logistics and everything else. In starting the process, I created the leverage of committing myself to taking the journey. A foot in the boat, the first rope cut from the dock. In the most impulsive, crazy, and important moment in saving my own life, I said yes to my gut instinct.

We were in escrow shortly thereafter and I was immediately lighter, buzzing with excitement for manufacturing an opportunity to do something completely new. And I was terrified out of my mind about how I'd leave Disney. How would I make a living in this new adventure we were jumping into? How well would I do in an environment where I had no experience?

As for Disney, I pled insanity to my amazing bosses who didn't understand the decision but supported it. To the question of making a living, it became trial by fire as we made a hundred mistakes for every brilliant idea. In the worry of how well I'd do, I did as well as I could. Start-up culture was jarring relative to corporate life, handing me a big serving of learning the hard way that required a lot of pivoting and even more humbling moments.

Stepping into the work of writing and teaching fueled my soul at the same rate it triggered my sense of normalcy. The vulnerability necessary was a wild departure from my past, the insecurities of doing it well ever-present.

This season of accelerated growth did see me falling victim to my negative thoughts and coping mechanisms in the turbulence of discomfort along the way. But ultimately it also saw in that human struggle an acclimation to the conditions at sea. Every day, more and more, I became the captain of my ship.

It started with the courage to say yes, the willingness to get radically self-aware, and the commitment to stay brave in the face of all of my greatest fears. The events of 2016 set the course, and in so many ways, the version of myself a year into the adventure wouldn't even recognize the version of who I was a year before I set sail. A testimony to the power of enduring the swells at sea.

The same can certainly be said for the past year of my life. As much as the end of my marriage a year ago was the introduction to discomfort I didn't choose and a push into a chaotic sea, it's still something I'll credit with saving my life, again. Not until I hit my lowest point did I ask what I'd do against that adversity. Not until I was forced to dig deep to understanding the role I played in the things that didn't work. Would I stay down or get up? I knew that getting up would require a deep inventory of what mattered and what no longer mattered at all.

That low point was also where an incredibly important yes was answered to the question: Will you choose to show up for your life? Courage can feel easier when it's a harbor we're deciding to leave, but life does not always give you a choice when it comes to when you'll be forced to brave the choppy water. Times will come when the sea chooses you, and the decision you'll have to make is if you believe enough in yourself and your calling to cultivate the courage to walk toward the scary unknown and rise through it, maybe even because of it.

Rachel and I had an extraordinary partnership over nearly two decades with so many incredible adventures that are trumped only by our four amazing kids. Her ability to see then what I can see now—that this decision will allow me to be the man I was meant to be, and her the woman she was meant to be—was an incredible gift. I mean, divorce sucks. I wish it on no one, would have fought for my entire life to not have one, and in this case, may have done so to keep myself in a harbor that would not have ever allowed the kind of abundance that will come for us individually or for our children who now benefit from us each as the very best versions of ourselves, showing up for them as even better parents. Thank you, Rae.

All three instances when I moved away from a harbor I knew for the choppy waters I needed required the cultivation of courage. The courage to face my fears. The courage to get back up. The courage to be patient when the wind wasn't blowing and the courage to hold on when it started to gust. The courage to believe enough in myself to think myself worthy of the audacity of my dreams and the courage to do so irrespective of what society, tradition, or any individual person might say.

That courage came through the process we've walked through in this book. If you're ready to live your full life, to step into who you were created to be, you must:

Have the courage to believe in yourself and believe you were created for an extraordinary purpose.

Have the courage to move ahead boldly, reinforcing the faith in your calling in a way that equips you to face your fears head-on.

Have the courage to see the experiences of your life as the qualifications for the vision you have of who you're becoming and the life you want.

Have the courage to be honest about what you'll need and where you struggle.

Have the courage to sail on your own map, even as it makes others uncomfortable, especially as it diverges from the safe route taken by people that are okay just being okay.

Have the courage to lean into your strengths in a way that fortifies you with a confidence to broaden what you define as strengths.

Have the courage to share your gifts with a world that so desperately needs them.

Have the courage to align the actions of your life with the values that you stand for.

Have the courage to set boundaries to keep those who would try to compromise that courage at bay.

Have the courage to truly, honestly know yourself in a way that affords you rapport and trust with the intuition that lives inside to guide you.

Have the courage to change.

Have the courage to question why you believe what you do about who you are, what you can do, and why you can do it.

Have the courage to challenge and reframe the limiting beliefs that might keep you tied to the dock.

Have the courage to create priorities that serve who you are and who you hope to be, even if those priorities make other people uncomfortable.

Have the courage to see the bright side, the hopefulness that exists for your future in a way that gets there because of, not in spite of, your past experiences or current conditions.

Have the courage to be your own best storyteller about those experiences of your past in how they were for you and qualify you completely for the ambition of what's ahead.

Have the courage to find the good in the hard and the growth that comes through pain.

Have the courage to see the thousands of micro-blessings around you every day, especially on the hard ones.

Have the courage to take ownership of this journey where you are the hero who saves themself.

Have the courage to push into hard conversations that question the systems and structures that make this journey harder for some than others.

Have the courage to appreciate that what currently is may not always be and let it catalyze you into action.

Have the courage to tend to your health, all of your healths, in a way that gives you a fighting chance to make it on the long voyage ahead.

Have the courage to focus on the essentials, and even more courage to let go of everything not on that list.

Have the courage to dream big and to have an imagination that allows your full potential to be realized.

Have the courage to be intentional with the work that's required to make that vision a reality.

Have the courage to bring your fears into the light.

Have the courage to walk toward your fear in a way that allows the exposure to it make you brave.

Have the courage to stop worrying about what other people think.

Have the courage to release yourself from what might happen since you have no control.

Have the courage to prepare for the things that can get in your way.

Have the courage to see the guarantee of death as a call for you to fight for your life.

Have the courage to depend on faith, the promise that what you need on this journey will be provided along the way.

Have the courage to seek out perspective from those who might, in their wisdom and experience, offer you some of their courage on the days when you're running low.

Have the courage to be disciplined for the work that lies ahead so that the full intention of your creator might avail itself through your commitment.

Have the courage to remain flexible with a journey that will require it.

Have the courage to fight for integrity in your life, that your actions on this, the only day you control, might align with the way you'd need to show up for the life you aspire to live.

Have the courage to say yes when your intuition begs you to listen to what it already knows you need.

Have the courage to grow by choosing to put yourself in discomfort.

Have the courage to give yourself grace along the way. You'll need it.

The tattoo on my right forearm still acts as a daily reminder that the only way I will ever feel a sense of fulfillment, a connection to my calling, the pride and peace that comes in actualizing my fullest potential is if I'm willing to put myself out on the choppy waters that will afford me the chance of getting there.

A ship in harbor is safe, but that's not what ships are built for.

I was built for this. So were you. Be courageous. It's time to leave the harbor.

A FINAL, IMPORTANT THOUGHT

NOT SURE THIS is the most conventional thing, but it's on my heart. I wrote the first chapter of a pitch for a future project based on my podcast, *Rise Together*, and have included it here as a post-conclusion close. The project is the attempt to take the stories, experiences, and lives of those who might look, live, and do differently than us and shine a light on them. The attempt to bring those stories to a broader audience in a way that affords an opportunity for empathy and understanding. The hope for softening the sharper edges of our hearts through compassion. Walking alongside someone who has the world receive them differently than it might you.

I originally wrote this chapter to fit in this book. The idea of having the courage to talk about hard stuff, the willingness to push into discomfort for the opportunity to grow, they align with the themes. But in a way that felt too lightly touched, shoehorned to fit, I decided instead to offer it here as an important and difficult challenge for any reader, and a way for me to be committed to continue doing the work of elevating the stories that need more oxygen. In this, the beginning of what's next, here's to the stories that need to be told. May we hear them, be challenged by them, be catalyzed into action and advocacy, in a way that allows us all to Rise Together.

The Moving Sidewalk

The first tattoo I got was the single word ALLY. It sits just below my elbow on my right forearm and acts as a reminder that *I'll stand with you and advocate for your worth*, especially if you don't have as loud a voice or enjoy the same access as I might as a white, straight, male, able-bodied American. I got the tattoo just after my biracial daughter was born. A year into attending an intentionally multicultural church that opened my eyes to so many things that only exist in doing life with those who've had a different experience from my own. I got it after watching my close gay friends shunned by that same church. I got it in the aftermath of a front-row glimpse into the fractured foster care system.

I also got it working in an industry that hadn't yet dealt with Harvey Weinstein. Sitting in board rooms where everyone for the most part looked like me. The beneficiary of nineteen promotions in my more than two decades in entertainment, I hadn't yet been forced to do the harder work of asking if it were possible that there were more qualified women, people of color, those with different backgrounds that may have been overlooked as I was moving ahead. Why there wasn't a broader, representative cross section sitting at my tables. I had much to learn. Still do.

At the time while working at Disney as the head of sales for the film studio, I felt good for leaning into opportunities as an executive advisor for a Black employee resource group, a Women@Disney initiative, and the role as "chief ally" for our Pride group, but those experiences were merely the tip of the iceberg in understanding the systems and structures that would reveal themselves in the four years since I got the tattoo. I can see now in some ways I was trading off showing up and leaning in for doing the more uncomfortable, nails-dirty work of confronting the systems and structures, actively pushing against the oppressive current.

Over the past several years, we've witnessed the protests and activism against racism via Black Lives Matter, the arrival of #MeToo and Time's Up movements fighting sexism and inequality against women, the significance of Supreme Court decisions to protect the civil liberties of gay and transgender people, the horrors of family separation at the southern borders, and the evidence of incredibly higher COVID death rates in high-poverty areas. These events have all brought into focus the systemic injustices that have existed for much of our country's history. All of them give an opportunity for each of us to own where we are.

As a person born in the US, I live in a country that has historically given advantage to certain members of society: white, straight, male, wealthy, born in this country. As a person who happens to check all of these boxes, *owning where I am,* means acknowledging something called *privilege.* As in, I have benefited from the systems, social constructs, and structures that make the journey ahead more challenging for my friends of color, women, those in the LGBTQ community, those with less financial means, or those who are foreign born. I don't like that these forces exist. It may make me uncomfortable at times to confront why they do or what I can do about it. But that they exist and that the inequities present in our world are real, it begs a question of what to do once you know.

As much as I touched on this concept in my first book, the events of the past two years have drawn even more light, brought more powerful and heartbreaking stories often amplified by social media to bear in a way that requires pushing into the uncomfortable. Listening, learning, creating an empathy bridge in community with people who've walked a different path that might catalyze our opportunity for advocacy. Hope for collectively becoming comfortable to challenge the systems that enable the inequity.

What I hope you'll find in the stories ahead is something of a challenge. A challenge particularly to any readers who benefit from privilege to own where *you* are. In my ongoing journey to do this, the first step has been to educate myself in an attempt to begin to understand the context and history of the systems that have afforded control of one group over another and that have contributed to my privilege. It is crucial for all of us to examine our privilege, and to look squarely at the reality that there are systemic issues that may allow some of us a smoother voyage than others. And as we recognize our privilege, we must also ask ourselves what we can do to correct our course, so that the wake of our privilege does not impede the journey of others. This is our responsibility as humans.

My last book was about having the courage to leave your safe harbor, and when it comes to the kinds of harbors we may need to leave, if you are someone who benefits from privilege, among the hardest to talk about, and the most important to address, are the systemic harbors that have oppressed people over time. Consider:

- *Racism.* The long-maintained structures in our society that have propped up and facilitated white supremacy and discrimination against people of color.
- *Sexism.* The dominance and violence asserted by men against women in a patriarchal society.
- *LGBTQ discrimination.* The history of hate and discrimination against those in our society who identify as gay or transgender.
- *Xenophobia.* The fear and hatred of, and discrimination against, the foreign-born in our society, often justified under the guise of nationalism.
- *Socioeconomic injustice.* The unequal access and services from one socioeconomic class to another.

The challenge is to create the empathy bridge so that you might be able to put yourself in someone else's shoes. It's an attempt to push outside our comfort zones, to walk into hard conversations, read books that will make us feel uncomfortable, get into community with people who will trigger some of our guilt reflexes, challenge why these structures exist, and ask better questions about how they can be addressed.

Our country as a whole is struggling with how to leave this harbor.

Once you see it, you can't unsee it.

On my podcast I recently interviewed Dr. Ed Barron, an expert in diversity and leadership with a specialty in understanding racism. In our conversation he cited a tipping point of the civil rights movement: the second crossing of the Edmund Pettus Bridge in Selma, Alabama, on what became known as Bloody Sunday. As Dr. Barron recounted, organizers of the movement knew they needed "conscious, courageous, white participants" to effect the change they needed. As history would have it, the events of March 7, 1965, in Selma were televised, bringing the reality of the struggle into homes, forcing onto white people, who'd enjoyed the privilege of a life free from discrimination, the responsibility of deciding what they should do now that they had seen what they couldn't unsee.

Dr. Barron went on to tell the story of sociologist Beverly Daniel Tatum who is credited with having described us all as having been born into a society and placed on a moving sidewalk of racism. She doesn't attempt to argue that there is racism because that's a given, but what she does say is that unless you turn around and start walking intentionally and vigorously against that moving sidewalk, then you're going with the flow (the systems, structures, and broader societal constructs) that supports racism. There is no neutral.

I'll argue that the observations that Dr. Tatum makes about racism hold for all forms of supremacy that might look to hold back women, discriminate based on sexual orientation, inequitably serve the poor, or mistreat the foreign-born.

The idea that there's no neutral is triggering, particularly if you're someone in the majority. I'm sure someone reading this right now is already writing a letter because the assertion here is that it's not enough to say that you're not racist, that you support women's rights, or that you're an ally to the LGBTQ community. Not actively participating in hate crimes or calling people the n-word or discriminating against anyone intentionally *is neutral*, because the opposite of doing those things isn't not doing them. It's actively resisting them. It's not enough to say I'm not racist. You have to do the work. You see, when you aren't actively resisting, as uncomfortable as this may make you feel, you're passively participating.

Those may be fightin' words to some of you, but I believe in a God who created humans in His image. Not just humans who live in certain countries, who have a certain color of skin, gender, amount of money, or anything else. All humans. That any one group may suffer the injustices of discrimination or supremacy at the hands of another is something that frankly is worth getting uncomfortable over, pushing out into the choppy waters of having to understand where these systemic issues come from, in the attempt to create momentum in the opposite direction and dismantle the structures that allow the injustice in the first place.

"Love your neighbor as yourself."

—MARK 12:31

"For God does not show favoritism."
—ROMANS 2:11

"When a foreigner resides among you in your land,
do not mistreat them."
—LEVITICUS 19:33

"So in Christ Jesus you are all children of God through faith."
—GALATIANS 3:26

Dr. Barron ended our conversation with a nod to Dr. Martin Luther King Jr's quote "Injustice anywhere is a threat to justice everywhere," a recognition that the issues of inequity don't only affect the oppressed, they affect humanity. These issues affect us all.

Having seen what we have, knowing things we can't unknow, the challenge is to disrupt our comfort. To look deeper into something that we may have previously tried to avoid having to really look at, particularly if you identify as someone of privilege, someone in the majority. That might mean investing time in the books, documentaries, podcasts, and articles that provide deeper context and detail around these systems and structures so that, in understanding them better, you might be armed to ask better questions. Think differently about policy. Appreciate the opportunities for advocacy.

Owning where you are comes with the responsibility to do something with what you've come to own. When you can accept why and how injustice and privilege exist, that's where the work really begins.

It will not be easy work to intentionally challenge the things that many of us were taught, the beliefs of our family of origin, the often unconscious current that we all find ourselves floating on. It will not be easy, but leaving this harbor for the discomfort of the open seas where we confront these systems and structures is work that all of us must do for the sake of humanity.

Every day I'm taking small steps on a never-ending journey to try to better understand these systemic issues, the groups they affect, the policies and structures that reinforce them, and the privilege that comes to someone like me as a by-product. It requires courage to acknowledge that you will not get it right. It takes humility to appreciate that it's something that you will never fully understand if you aren't among the disenfranchised. It's uncomfortable, hard work. But it's nothing compared to how I imagine the experience of someone trying to reach for a better life against oppressive headwinds that have existed since the beginning of time.

LOGBOOK

JOURNALING ACTIVITY

If you're interested in doing the hard work of understanding systemic oppression and unraveling your privilege and how you fit in, I encourage you to start by reading as much as you can on the subject. Have the courage to get uncomfortable and to challenge some of your current beliefs by hearing an alternative perspective. Here is my recommended read and watch list for getting started:

- *How to Be an Antiracist* by Ibram X. Kendi: Kendi identifies and describes racism and makes a case for why we must actively do the work to dismantle it in our everyday lives.
- *Between the World and Me* by Ta-Nehisi Coates: Coates offers a powerful framework to understand the context between the country's history around race and how it plays into the current crisis.
- *White Fragility* by Robin DiAngelo: DiAngelo writes about why it's so hard for white people to talk about racism.
- *We Should All Be Feminists* by Chimamanda Ngozi Adichie: Adichie eloquently introduces a unique conversation around feminism for this century rooted in inclusion and awareness.
- *Caste* by Isabel Wilkerson: Wilkerson offers insight into the hierarchical human ranking system that exists in

American society, with a vision for how we can move forward as a country.

- *Unclobber* by Colby Martin: Martin examines what the Bible says (and does not say) about homosexuality in a way that challenges outdated and inaccurate assumptions and interpretations.
- Consider watching Ava DuVernay's *13th*, Raoul Peck's *I Am Not Your Negro*, Davis Guggenheim's *He Named Me Malala*, and the Netflix docuseries *Immigration Nation*.

ACKNOWLEDGMENTS

I want to start by thanking God for the opportunity to do this work. For the blessings and growth that came in a hard season. For the way His love showed up over and over again through strangers, authors, friends, and family along the way.

Thanks to you, this community, who have been such an incredible source of encouragement and strength, especially on the tougher days. I'll spend the rest of my life repaying the debt through my work, and bad jokes.

Thank you to Jeff, Jamie, Becky, Sara, and your teams at HarperCollins Leadership. To Kevan Lyon for so much support.

Thank you to Brady and Lynn, Paul, the entire PR Beachgang, Jason the pastor, David the therapist, Chris and Susan, Trey and Jenny, Brad and Chris, and the rest of my friends who were there when I needed you most.

To my parents—thank you for always being there for me. Heather and Chuck, Andy and Erin, Tim and Kirsten, and all of your 1,000 kids—I love you.

Jackson, Sawyer, Ford, and Noah—being your father is among the greatest accomplishments of my lifetime. I love you each more than I could ever fully express.

And to Heidi, thank you for being such a miracle in this past year. Your empathy, kindness, and friendship were a lifeline beyond anything I could have wished for. Your belief in the good things to come made me a believer. You've given me far more than you can ever fully appreciate, and I will be indebted forever.

INDEX

ABOUT THE AUTHOR

DAD OF FOUR RAD KIDS,
NEW YORK TIMES BESTSELLING AUTHOR,
COACH, PODCAST HOST, SPEAKER,
RUNNER, AND ALLY

DAVE HOLLIS'S purpose on this planet is to encourage people to step toward their calling while equipping them with the tools to lead an exceptional life.

Dave is a *New York Times* bestselling author, host of the popular *Rise Together* podcast, keynote speaker, and life and business coach. Dave's history includes serving as CEO of a media start-up, president of sales for the film studio at The Walt Disney Company, and a talent manager across film, television, and music, along with work in publicity, research, and technology in the entertainment sector.

Dave is the father to four kids, a four-time foster parent, an avid runner, a sports memorabilia enthusiast, and the proud owner of a 1969 Ford Bronco.

A portion of the proceeds from this book will go to the Hollis Giving Fund, Dave's philanthropic vehicle, which focuses on the needs of children in foster care, teen homelessness, and food insecurity.

Dave has sat on the board of the membership committee for the Academy of Motion Pictures, Arts, and Sciences, of which he is a member, and on the boards of Fandango Labs, Will Rogers Motion Picture Pioneers, National Angels, and his alma mater Pepperdine's Institute for Entertainment Media and Culture.

His upcoming projects include the launch of a *Teatime with Noah* children's book series with the debut *Here's to Your Dreams!*, the expansion of Congruent Conference, a men's growth and development event, a health and fitness portfolio with his partner Heidi Lane Powell, additional podcast offerings, ever-evolving coaching programs, and more. To become engaged in the community and learn more, visit mrdavehollis.com.